Macaroni & Cheese
101 recipes

D0904708

pil

Publications International, Ltd.

Recipe development on pages 66, 70, 84 and 114 by Bev Bennett.
Recipe development on pages 8, 16, 74 and 94 by Marilyn Pocius.

Front cover photography and photography on pages 9, 17, 67, 71, 75, 85, 95 and 115 by PIL Photo Studio.
Photographer: Tate Hunt
Photographer's Assistant: Justin Paris
Food Stylists: Janice Bell, Kim Hartman
Assistant Food Stylists: Elaine Funk, Marena Upton

Pictured on the front cover: Mac & Cheesiest *(page 8)*.
Pictured on the back cover *(left to right):* Mediterranean Mac & Cheese *(page 94)* and Mac & Cheese Pizza *(page 114)*.

ISBN-13: 975-1-4508-2161-2
ISBN-10: 1-4508-2161-8

Library of Congress Control Number: 2011921600

Manufactured in China.

8 7 6 5 4 3 2 1

Microwave Cooking: Microwave ovens vary in wattage. Use the cooking times as guidelines and check for doneness before adding more time.

Preparation/Cooking Times: Preparation times are based on the approximate amount of time required to assemble the recipe before cooking, baking, chilling or serving. These times include preparation steps such as measuring, chopping and mixing. The fact that some preparations and cooking can be done simultaneously is taken into account. Preparation of optional ingredients and serving suggestions is not included.

Publications International, Ltd.

table of contents

Classic Casseroles 4

Meaty Mac.. 28

Veggie Versions... 50

Ethnic Twists...74

Family Favorites 100

Easy & Cheesy 120

Acknowledgments 141

Index...142

veggie mac and tuna
page 108

tomato, brie & noodle casserole
page 84

classic casseroles

classic macaroni and cheese
makes 6 servings

- 3 tablespoons butter or margarine
- ¼ cup finely chopped onion (optional)
- 2 tablespoons all-purpose flour
- ½ teaspoon salt
- ⅛ teaspoon black pepper
- 2 cups milk
- 2 cups (8 ounces) SARGENTO® Fancy Shredded Mild Cheddar Cheese, divided
- 2 cups elbow macaroni, cooked and drained

MELT butter in medium saucepan over medium heat. Cook onion, if desired, in butter 5 minutes or until tender. Stir in flour, salt and pepper. Gradually add milk and cook, stirring occasionally, until thickened.

REMOVE from heat. Add 1½ cups cheese and stir until cheese is melted. Combine cheese sauce with cooked macaroni. Place in 1½-quart casserole; top with remaining cheese.

BAKE in preheated 350°F oven 30 minutes or until bubbly and cheese is lightly browned.

prep time: 15 minutes • **cook time:** 30 minutes

macaroni & cheese with bacon & tomatoes

makes 6 servings

    4 thick slices applewood smoked bacon, diced
    2 tablespoons all-purpose flour
 2¼ cups milk
    ½ teaspoon salt
    ⅛ teaspoon cayenne pepper
1¾ cups (7 ounces) SARGENTO® Shredded Colby-Jack Cheese, divided
    8 ounces (2 cups dry) multi-grain or regular elbow macaroni, cooked and drained
    1 can (14 ounces) fire-roasted diced tomatoes, drained

COOK bacon in a large saucepan over medium heat 5 to 6 minutes or until crisp, stirring frequently. Use a slotted spoon to transfer bacon to a paper towel; set aside.

ADD flour to drippings in pan; cook and stir 30 seconds. Add milk, salt and cayenne pepper; bring to a boil. Simmer 1 minute or until sauce thickens, stirring frequently. Remove from heat; stir in 1¼ cups cheese until melted. Stir in cooked macaroni and tomatoes. Transfer to a sprayed 9-inch baking dish or shallow 1½-quart casserole.

BAKE in a preheated 375°F oven 20 minutes or until heated through. Sprinkle reserved bacon and remaining cheese over macaroni; continue to bake 5 minutes or until cheese is melted.

prep time: 15 minutes • **cook time:** 25 minutes

cheddar tuna noodles
makes 4 to 6 servings

2 tablespoons butter
½ cup chopped onion
½ cup chopped celery
2 tablespoons all-purpose flour
½ teaspoon salt
¼ teaspoon red pepper flakes
2 cups milk
8 ounces egg noodles, cooked and drained
2 cans (6 ounces each) white tuna packed in water, drained and flaked
1 cup frozen peas
½ cup (2 ounces) shredded Cheddar cheese

1. Preheat oven to 375°F. Lightly coat 9-inch square baking dish with nonstick cooking spray.

2. Melt butter in large skillet over medium heat. Add onion; cook and stir 3 minutes. Add celery; cook and stir 3 minutes.

3. Sprinkle flour, salt and red pepper flakes over onion mixture; cook and stir 2 minutes. Gradually whisk in milk; bring to a boil. Cook and stir 2 minutes or until thickened. Remove from heat.

4. Combine noodles, white sauce, tuna and peas in prepared baking dish; stir to coat. Sprinkle with cheese. Bake 20 to 25 minutes or until bubbly.

mac & cheesiest
makes about 6 servings

- **8 ounces uncooked elbow macaroni**
- **¼ cup (½ stick) butter**
- **5 tablespoons flour**
- **2¾ cups warm milk**
- **1 teaspoon salt**
- **¼ teaspoon ground nutmeg**
- **¼ teaspoon ground black pepper**
- **2 to 3 drops hot pepper sauce (optional)**
- **8 ounces (about 2 cups) shredded Cheddar cheese, divided**
- **2 ounces (about ½ cup) shredded Gruyère or Swiss cheese**
- **2 ounces (about ½ cup) shredded American cheese**
- **3 ounces (about ¾ cup) shredded aged Gouda cheese**

1. Preheat oven to 350°F. Cook pasta according to package directions until barely al dente. Run under cold running water to stop cooking; drain.

2. Melt butter in large saucepan or deep skillet over medium-low heat until bubbly. Whisk in flour until smooth paste forms; cook and stir 2 minutes without browning. Gradually whisk in milk over medium heat; cook 6 to 8 minutes, whisking constantly until mixture begins to bubble and thickens slightly. Add salt, nutmeg, black pepper and hot pepper sauce, if desired.

3. Remove pan from heat and stir in 1½ cups of Cheddar, Gruyère, American and Gouda cheeses. Stir until smooth. Stir pasta into cheese sauce. Transfer to 2-quart casserole dish; sprinkle with remaining ½ cup Cheddar cheese.

4. Bake 20 to 30 minutes or until golden and bubbly.

baked pasta and cheese supreme

makes 4 servings

    8 ounces uncooked fusilli pasta or other
        corkscrew-shaped pasta
    8 ounces uncooked bacon, diced
    ½ medium onion, chopped
    2 cloves garlic, minced
    2 teaspoons dried oregano, divided
    1 can (8 ounces) tomato sauce
    1 teaspoon hot pepper sauce (optional)
 1½ cups (6 ounces) shredded Cheddar or Colby cheese
    ½ cup fresh bread crumbs (from 1 slice of white bread)
    1 tablespoon melted butter

1. Preheat oven to 400°F. Cook pasta according to package directions; drain. Meanwhile, cook bacon in large ovenproof skillet over medium heat until crisp; drain and set aside.

2. Add onion, garlic and 1 teaspoon oregano to skillet; cook and stir about 3 minutes or until onion is translucent. Stir in tomato sauce and hot pepper sauce, if desired. Add cooked pasta and cheese to skillet; stir to coat.

3. Combine bacon, bread crumbs, remaining 1 teaspoon oregano and melted butter in small bowl; sprinkle over pasta mixture. Bake about 5 minutes or until hot and bubbly.

traditional macaroni & cheese

makes 6 servings

   2 tablespoons cornstarch
   1 teaspoon salt
   ½ teaspoon dry mustard
   ¼ teaspoon ground black pepper
   **1 can (12 fluid ounces) NESTLÉ®
      CARNATION® Evaporated Milk**
   1 cup water
   2 tablespoons butter or margarine
   2 cups (8 ounces) shredded sharp cheddar cheese, divided
**1⅔ cups (about 7 ounces) dry small elbow macaroni, cooked and
      drained**

PREHEAT oven to 375°F. Grease 2-quart casserole dish.

COMBINE cornstarch, salt, mustard and pepper in medium saucepan. Stir in evaporated milk, water and butter. Cook over medium-heat, stirring constantly, until mixture comes to a boil. Boil for 1 minute. Remove from heat. Stir in 1½ cups cheese until melted. Add macaroni; mix well. Pour into prepared casserole dish. Top with remaining cheese.

BAKE for 20 to 25 minutes or until cheese is melted and light brown.

tip: To transform Macaroni & Cheese from a simple dish to a savory one-dish meal, add 1 cup chopped ham or hot dogs after milk mixture comes to a boil.

macaroni and cheese dijon
makes 6 servings

- 1¼ cups milk
- ½ pound (8 ounces) VELVEETA® Pasteurized Prepared Cheese Product, cut into ½-inch cubes
- 2 tablespoons GREY POUPON® Dijon Mustard
- 3½ cups tri-colored rotini pasta, cooked, drained
- 6 slices OSCAR MAYER® Bacon, cooked, drained and crumbled
- ⅓ cup green onion slices
- ⅛ teaspoon ground red pepper (cayenne)
- ½ cup French fried onion rings

1. HEAT oven to 350°F. Mix milk, VELVEETA® and mustard in medium saucepan on low heat until VELVEETA® is completely melted and mixture is well blended, stirring occasionally. Add pasta, bacon, green onions and pepper; mix lightly.

2. SPOON into greased 2-quart casserole dish; cover.

3. BAKE 15 to 20 minutes or until heated through; stir. Top with onions. Bake, uncovered, 5 minutes. Let stand 10 minutes before serving.

tip: For easy crumbled bacon, use kitchen scissors to snip raw bacon into ½-inch pieces. Let pieces fall right into skillet, then cook until crisp and drain on paper towels.

prep time: 20 minutes • **total time:** 45 minutes

roasted garlic & stout mac & cheese
makes 8 to 10 servings

1 head garlic
1 tablespoon olive oil
6 tablespoons butter, divided
1 cup panko bread crumbs
¼ cup all-purpose flour
1 teaspoon salt, divided
½ teaspoon black pepper
2 cups whole milk
¾ cup Irish stout
2 cups (8 ounces) shredded sharp Cheddar cheese
2 cups (8 ounces) shredded Dubliner cheese
1 pound cavatappi or penne pasta, cooked and drained

1. Preheat oven to 375°F. Butter shallow 4-quart baking dish.

2. Cut ½ inch off pointed top of garlic bulb to expose cloves. Drizzle with oil; wrap in foil. Bake 30 to 45 minutes or until softened. When cool, squeeze cloves into small bowl. Mash with fork; set aside.

3. Melt 2 tablespoons butter. Toss with bread crumbs in medium bowl; set aside.

4. Melt remaining 4 tablespoons butter in large saucepan over medium-low heat. Whisk in flour until smooth paste forms; cook and stir 2 minutes without browning. Stir in roasted garlic paste, salt and pepper. Gradually whisk in milk and stout. Raise heat to medium-high; cook 6 to 8 minutes, whisking constantly until mixture thickens slightly. Remove from heat; gradually stir in cheeses.

5. Combine cheese sauce with pasta in large bowl. Transfer to prepared baking dish; sprinkle with bread crumbs. Bake 40 minutes or until golden brown and bubbly.

confetti mac & cheese

makes 4 servings

1½ cups uncooked elbow macaroni
1 cup chopped onion
1 cup chopped red or green bell pepper
¾ cup chopped celery
1 cup SARGENTO® Ricotta Cheese
1 cup (4 ounces) SARGENTO® ARTISAN BLENDS™ Shredded Swiss Cheese
½ cup (2 ounces) SARGENTO® Shredded Mild Cheddar Cheese
½ cup milk
3 egg whites
3 tablespoons all-purpose flour
1 tablespoon butter
½ teaspoon salt
¼ teaspoon black pepper
¼ teaspoon hot pepper sauce

PREHEAT oven to 350°F. Coat 2-quart casserole with nonstick cooking spray; set aside. Prepare macaroni according to package directions, omitting salt. During last 5 minutes of cooking add onion, bell pepper and celery. Drain pasta and vegetables.

WHILE macaroni is cooking, combine Ricotta, Swiss, Cheddar, milk, egg whites, flour, butter, salt, black pepper and pepper sauce in food processor or blender; process until smooth. Stir cheese mixture into pasta and vegetables.

POUR mixture into prepared casserole. Bake 35 to 40 minutes or until golden brown. Let stand 10 minutes before serving.

prep time: 10 minutes • **cook time:** 50 minutes

cheddar & cavatappi
makes 4 to 6 servings

  8 ounces uncooked whole wheat cavatappi pasta (about 3 cups)
  6 tablespoons butter, divided
  3 shallots, thinly sliced
  5 tablespoons flour
  1 cup milk
  1 cup whipping cream
  ½ teaspoon salt
  ½ teaspoon dry mustard
  2 drops hot pepper sauce (optional)
  3 cups (12 ounces) shredded Cheddar cheese
  1 cup peas
  ¼ cup dry bread crumbs

1. Preheat oven to 350°F. Cook pasta according to package directions until barely al dente. Run under cold running water to stop cooking; drain.

2. Meanwhile, melt 1 tablespoon butter in medium skillet over low heat. Add shallots; cook and stir 5 to 7 minutes or until well browned. Remove from heat.

3. Melt 4 tablespoons butter in large saucepan or deep skillet over medium heat until bubbly. Whisk in flour until smooth paste forms; cook and stir 2 minutes without browning. Gradually whisk in milk and cream over medium heat; cook 6 to 8 minutes, whisking frequently until mixture begins to bubble and thickens. Stir in salt, mustard and hot pepper sauce.

4. Turn heat to low; gradually stir in Cheddar cheese until melted. Remove from heat. Stir in pasta, shallots and peas.

5. Transfer to 1½-quart casserole; sprinkle with bread crumbs. Bake 20 to 25 minutes or until hot and bubbly.

three-cheese chicken penne pasta bake

makes 4 servings

1½ cups multi-grain penne pasta, uncooked
1 package (9 ounces) fresh spinach leaves
1 pound boneless skinless chicken breasts, cut into bite-size pieces
1 teaspoon dried basil leaves
1 jar (14½ ounce) spaghetti sauce
1 can (14½ ounce) diced tomatoes, drained
2 ounces (¼ of 8-ounce package) PHILADELPHIA® ⅓ Less Fat than Cream Cheese, cubed
1 cup KRAFT® 2% Milk Shredded Mozzarella Cheese, divided
2 tablespoons KRAFT® Grated Parmesan Cheese

1. HEAT oven to 375°F.

2. COOK pasta as directed on package, adding spinach to the boiling water the last minute.

3. COOK and stir chicken and basil in large nonstick skillet sprayed with cooking spray on medium-high heat 3 minutes. Stir in spaghetti sauce and tomatoes; bring to boil. Simmer on low heat 3 minutes or until chicken is done. Stir in cream cheese.

4. DRAIN pasta mixture; return to pan. Stir in chicken mixture and ½ cup mozzarella. Spoon into 2-quart casserole or 8-inch square baking dish.

5. BAKE 20 minutes. Sprinkle with remaining cheeses. Bake 3 minutes.

serving suggestion: Serve with CRYSTAL LIGHT® Iced Tea. Nutrition Bonus: A variety of cheese adds great flavor to this low-calorie meal that is rich in vitamin A from the spinach.

prep time: 20 minutes • **total time:** 43 minutes

southwestern mac and cheese
makes 6 servings

8 ounces uncooked elbow macaroni
1 can (about 14 ounces) diced tomatoes
with green peppers and onions
1 can (10 ounces) diced tomatoes with
green chiles
1½ cups salsa
3 cups (12 ounces) shredded Mexican cheese blend, divided

slow cooker directions

1. Lightly coat inside of slow cooker with nonstick cooking spray. Stir together macaroni, tomatoes, salsa and 2 cups cheese in prepared slow cooker. Cover; cook on LOW 3 hours and 45 minutes or until macaroni is tender.

2. Sprinkle remaining 1 cup cheese over macaroni and cheese in slow cooker. Cover; cook 15 minutes more or until cheese melts.

baked ziti

makes 8 servings

REYNOLDS WRAP® Non-Stick Foil
1 **pound ground beef, browned and drained**
4 **cups (32-ounce jar) chunky garden-style pasta sauce**
1 **tablespoon Italian seasoning, divided**
1 **package (16 ounces) ziti pasta, cooked and drained**
1 **package (8 ounces) shredded mozzarella cheese, divided**
1 **container (16 ounces) ricotta cheese or cottage cheese**
1 **egg**
¼ **cup grated Parmesan cheese, divided**

Preheat oven to 350°F.

Combine ground beef, pasta sauce and 2 teaspoons Italian seasoning. Stir pasta into meat sauce; spread half of mixture evenly in large baking pan. Top with half of mozzarella cheese.

Combine ricotta cheese, egg, 2 tablespoons Parmesan cheese and remaining Italian seasoning; spread over mozzarella cheese in pan. Spread remaining pasta mixture over ricotta cheese mixture. Sprinkle with remaining mozzarella and Parmesan cheeses.

Cover with REYNOLDS WRAP® Non-Stick Foil with non-stick (dull) side toward food.

Bake 45 minutes. Remove foil and continue baking 15 minutes or until cheese is melted and lightly browned. Let stand 15 minutes before serving.

prep time: 20 minutes • **cook time:** 1 hour

velveeta® down-home macaroni & cheese
makes 5 servings

¼ **cup (½ stick) butter or margarine, divided**
¼ **cup all-purpose flour**
 1 **cup milk**
½ **pound (8 ounces) VELVEETA® Pasteurized Prepared Cheese Product, cut into ½-inch cubes**
 2 **cups elbow macaroni, cooked, drained**
½ **cup KRAFT® Shredded Cheddar Cheese**
¼ **cup crushed RITZ® Crackers**

1. HEAT oven to 350°F. Melt 3 tablespoons butter in medium saucepan on medium heat. Whisk in flour; mix well. Cook 2 minutes, stirring constantly. Gradually stir in milk; cook until mixture boils and thickens, stirring constantly. Add VELVEETA®; cook until melted, stirring frequently. Stir in macaroni.

2. SPOON into 2-quart casserole sprayed with cooking spray; sprinkle with Cheddar. Melt remaining butter; toss with cracker crumbs. Sprinkle over casserole.

3. BAKE 20 minutes or until heated through.

healthy living: Save 60 calories, 9 grams fat, and 5 grams saturated fat per serving by preparing with fat-free milk, VELVEETA® Made With 2% Milk Reduced Fat Pasteurized Prepared Cheese Product, KRAFT® 2% Milk Shredded Reduced Fat Cheddar Cheese and RITZ® Reduced Fat Crackers.

jazz it up: Stir in ¼ cup OSCAR MAYER® Real Bacon Bits with the cooked macaroni.

prep time: 20 minutes • **total time:** 40 minutes

pepper jack cheesy mac
makes 6 servings

2 cups (8 ounces) dry elbow macaroni
2 cups (8-ounce package) shredded
    cheddar cheese
2 cups (8 ounces) shredded Pepper Jack
    cheese, divided
1 can (12 fluid ounces) NESTLÉ®
    CARNATION® Evaporated Milk
½ teaspoon ground black pepper
½ to 1 cup broken tortilla chips (your choice of color)
¼ to ½ teaspoon crushed red pepper (optional)

PREHEAT oven to 350°F. Lightly grease 2½-quart casserole dish.

COOK macaroni in large saucepan according to package directions; drain. Return to saucepan.

ADD cheddar cheese, *1½ cups* Pepper Jack cheese, evaporated milk and black pepper to macaroni; stir until combined. Pour into prepared casserole dish. Combine *remaining ½ cup* Pepper Jack cheese, tortilla chips and red pepper flakes in small bowl. Sprinkle over top. Cover tightly with foil.

BAKE for 20 minutes. Uncover; bake for an additional 10 minutes or until lightly browned.

home-style macaroni and cheese
makes 4 servings

        Nonstick cooking spray
    10 ounces uncooked elbow macaroni
    ¼ cup dry bread crumbs
     2 tablespoons chopped fresh parsley
     1 tablespoon grated Parmesan cheese
    ¼ teaspoon dried oregano
     6 ounces pasteurized process cheese product, cut into ½-inch
        cubes
     1 cup milk
     2 egg whites
    ¼ teaspoon salt
    ¼ teaspoon black pepper
     3 plum tomatoes, cut crosswise into ⅛-inch rounds

1. Preheat oven to 325°F. Spray 9-inch square baking pan with nonstick cooking spray.

2. Cook pasta according to package directions; drain. Place pasta in prepared pan.

3. Combine bread crumbs, parsley, Parmesan cheese and oregano in small bowl; set aside.

4. Combine cheese and milk in medium saucepan. Cook over medium heat until cheese melts, stirring constantly. Remove from heat; whisk in egg whites, salt and pepper until completely blended. Pour over pasta.

5. Arrange tomato slices on top of pasta; sprinkle evenly with bread crumb mixture. Lightly spray with nonstick cooking spray. Bake 35 minutes or until heated through. Let stand 5 minutes before serving.

tip: For a spicier dish use pasteurized process cheese spread with mild jalapeño peppers.

3-cheese pasta bake
makes 4 servings

1 can (10¾ ounces) CAMPBELL'S®
Condensed Cream of Mushroom Soup
(Regular or 98% Fat Free)

1 package (8 ounces) shredded two-
cheese blend (about 2 cups)

⅓ cup grated Parmesan cheese

1 cup milk

¼ teaspoon ground black pepper

3 cups corkscrew-shaped pasta, cooked and drained

1. Stir the soup, cheeses, milk and black pepper in a 1½-quart casserole. Stir in the pasta.

2. Bake at 400°F. for 20 minutes or until the mixture is hot and bubbling.

kitchen tip: Substitute 2 cups of your favorite shredded cheese for the two-cheese blend.

serving suggestion: Serve with a Caesar salad. For dessert serve red grapes.

prep time: 20 minutes • **bake time:** 20 minutes

veg•all® beef & cheddar bake

makes 4 to 6 servings

**2 cans (15 ounces each) VEG•ALL®
Original Mixed Vegetables, drained**

3 cups shredded Cheddar cheese

2 cups cooked elbow macaroni

**1 pound extra-lean ground beef, cooked
and drained**

½ cup chopped onion

¼ teaspoon black pepper

1. Preheat oven to 350°F.

2. In large mixing bowl, combine Veg•All, cheese, macaroni, ground beef, onion and pepper; mix well. Pour mixture into large casserole.

3. Bake for 30 to 35 minutes. Serve hot.

meaty mac

beef, bean and pasta casserole
makes 6 servings

- 2¾ cups uncooked whole wheat rigatoni
- 1 pound ground beef
- 1 medium onion, diced
- 2 cloves garlic, minced
- 1 can (about 15 ounces) cannellini beans, rinsed and drained
- 1 can (about 14 ounces) diced tomatoes, drained
- 1 can (8 ounces) tomato sauce
- 2 teaspoons Italian seasoning
- ½ to ¾ teaspoon salt (optional)
- ¼ teaspoon black pepper
- 1 cup finely shredded Parmesan cheese
- 1 cup (4 ounces) shredded mozzarella cheese

1. Preheat oven to 350°F. Lightly spray 11×7-inch baking dish with nonstick cooking spray. Cook pasta according to package directions; drain. Set aside.

2. Meanwhile, place beef, onion and garlic in large nonstick skillet. Brown beef over medium-high heat about 6 to 8 minutes, stirring to break up meat. Drain fat. Add beans, tomatoes, tomato sauce, Italian seasoning, salt and pepper; cook 3 minutes.

3. Remove skillet from heat; stir in cooked pasta and Parmesan cheese. Transfer mixture to prepared dish; sprinkle with mozzarella cheese. Bake 20 minutes or until casserole is bubbly and cheese is melted.

variations: Any short-shape pasta can be used in this recipe. Red kidney beans can be used instead of the cannellini, if desired.

prep time: 15 minutes • **cook/bake time:** 30 minutes

spicy ham & cheese pasta
makes 4 servings

- ½ (16-ounce) package corkscrew pasta
- 2 tablespoons olive oil
- 1 large red pepper, cut into julienne strips
- 1 small red onion, diced
- 1 large clove garlic, crushed
- 8 ounces cooked ham, cut into ½-inch cubes
- 1 cup ricotta cheese
- 3 tablespoons chopped parsley
- 1 teaspoon Original TABASCO® brand Pepper Sauce
- ¾ teaspoon salt

Prepare pasta according to package directions; drain. Heat oil in 10-inch skillet over medium heat; cook red pepper, onion and garlic until tender-crisp, about 5 minutes. Add ham cubes; cook 3 minutes longer, stirring occasionally.

Toss cooked pasta with ham mixture, ricotta cheese, parsley, TABASCO® Sauce and salt in large bowl; mix well.

kielbasa and broccoli linguine

makes 8 servings

1 package **HILLSHIRE FARM®** Polska Kielbasa
1 package (16 ounces) uncooked linguine
4 cups fresh small broccoli florets
½ cup chopped white onion
1 teaspoon hot sauce
1 package (7 ounces) refrigerated basil pesto
1 package (5 ounces) crumbled Gorgonzola cheese
2 green onions, sliced
Salt and ground black pepper to taste

1. Cook linguine according to package directions. During the last 4 minutes of cooking, add broccoli to water. When linguine and broccoli are tender, drain; keep warm.

2. Cut sausage in ½-inch cubes. Heat a 4- to 6-quart pan over medium-high heat for 3 minutes. Add sausage and onion to pan; cook 3 to 4 minutes, stirring occasionally until sausage is browned and onion is tender.

3. Add hot sauce, cooked linguine and broccoli. Toss gently over medium heat for 1 minute. Stir in pesto, Gorgonzola and green onions; heat through. Add salt and pepper to taste.

hearty beef lasagna

makes 8 to 10 servings

1 pound ground beef
1 jar (32 ounces) pasta sauce
2 cups (16 ounces) cottage cheese
1 container (8 ounces) sour cream
8 uncooked lasagna noodles
3 cups (12 ounces) shredded mozzarella cheese, divided
½ cup grated Parmesan cheese
1 cup water
Fresh basil or thyme (optional)

1. Preheat oven to 350°F.

2. Brown beef in large skillet over medium-high heat 6 to 8 minutes, stirring to break up meat. Drain fat. Add pasta sauce. Reduce heat to low, stirring occasionally until heated through. Combine cottage cheese and sour cream in medium bowl; blend well.

3. Spread 1½ cups meat sauce in 13×9-inch baking pan. Place 4 uncooked noodles over sauce. Top with half of cheese mixture, 1 cup of mozzarella cheese, half of remaining meat sauce and ¼ cup of Parmesan cheese. Repeat layers starting with uncooked noodles. Top with remaining 1 cup mozzarella cheese. Pour water into pan around sides. Cover tightly with foil.

4. Bake 1 hour. Uncover; bake 20 minutes or until hot and bubbly. Let stand 15 to 20 minutes before cutting. Garnish with basil.

wisconsin swiss ham and noodles casserole

makes 6 to 8 servings

- **2 tablespoons butter**
- **½ cup chopped onion**
- **½ cup chopped green bell pepper**
- **1 can (10½ ounces) condensed cream of mushroom soup**
- **1 cup dairy sour cream**
- **1 package (8 ounces) medium noodles, cooked and drained**
- **2 cups (8 ounces) shredded Wisconsin Swiss cheese**
- **2 cups cubed cooked ham (about ¾ pound)**

In 1-quart saucepan, melt butter; sauté onion and bell pepper. Remove from heat; stir in soup and sour cream. In buttered 2-quart casserole, layer ⅓ of the noodles, ⅓ of the Swiss cheese, ⅓ of the ham and ½ soup mixture. Repeat layers, ending with final ⅓ layer of noodles, cheese and ham. Bake in preheated 350°F oven 30 to 45 minutes or until heated through.

*Favorite recipe from **Wisconsin Milk Marketing Board***

cheddar brat mac and cheese

makes 5 servings

1 package (19.76 ounces) JOHNSONVILLE® Cheddar Bratwurst
1 package (16 ounces) elbow macaroni
1 jar (23 ounces) salsa con queso
1 cup cubed sharp cheddar cheese
½ cup water
1 teaspoon ground cumin
⅛ teaspoon cayenne pepper
¾ cup shredded pepper Jack cheese
3 green onions, sliced (optional)

Preheat grill to medium-low heat. Grill brats according to package directions; cut into ½-inch slices. Cook macaroni according to package directions for firm pasta.

In a large disposable foil pan, combine the salsa con queso, cheddar cheese, water, cumin and cayenne. Stir in brats and macaroni. Sprinkle with pepper Jack cheese and green onions. Place on the grill; cover with foil. Grill for 15 to 20 minutes or until hot.

tip: To add a smoky flavor, add 3 cups of wood chips (that have soaked in water) to the grill.

chili spaghetti casserole
makes 8 servings

  8 ounces uncooked spaghetti
  1 pound ground beef
  1 medium onion, chopped
  ¼ teaspoon salt
  ⅛ teaspoon black pepper
  1 can (15 ounces) vegetarian chili with beans
  1 can (14½ ounces) Italian-style stewed tomatoes, undrained
  1½ cups (6 ounces) shredded sharp Cheddar cheese, divided
  ½ cup sour cream
  1½ teaspoons chili powder
  ¼ teaspoon garlic powder

1. Preheat oven to 350°F. Spray 13×9-inch baking dish with nonstick cooking spray.

2. Cook pasta according to package directions. Drain and place in prepared dish.

3. Meanwhile, place beef and onion in large skillet; season with salt and pepper. Brown beef 6 to 8 minutes over medium-high heat, stirring to separate meat. Drain fat. Stir in chili, tomatoes with juice, 1 cup cheese, sour cream, chili powder and garlic powder.

4. Add chili mixture to pasta; stir until pasta is well coated. Sprinkle with remaining ½ cup cheese.

5. Cover tightly with foil and bake 30 minutes or until hot and bubbly. Let stand 5 minutes before serving.

spicy chili mac
makes 8 to 10 servings

- **¾ cup dried pinto beans**
- **¾ cup dried red kidney beans**
- **4 to 5 cups water plus additional for soaking beans**
- **1 pound ground beef or ground turkey**
- **2 cans (about 14 ounces each) diced tomatoes with green chilies**
- **1 package (about 1 ounce) chili seasoning mix**
- **2 tablespoons minced onion**
- **2 teaspoons beef bouillon granules**
- **¼ teaspoon red pepper flakes**
- **1½ cups uncooked rotini pasta**
- **2 cups (8 ounces) shredded Cheddar cheese**

1. Place beans in large bowl; cover with water. Soak 6 to 8 hours or overnight. (To quick soak beans, place in large saucepan; cover with water. Bring to a boil over high heat. Boil 2 minutes. Remove from heat; let soak, covered, 1 hour.) Drain beans; discard water.

2. Brown beef 6 to 8 minutes in large skillet over medium-high heat, stirring to break up meat. Drain fat. Combine beef, beans, 4 to 5 cups water, tomatoes, chili seasoning, onion, bouillon granules and pepper flakes in large saucepan or Dutch oven.

3. Bring to a boil over high heat. Cover; reduce heat and simmer 1½ hours or until beans are tender.

4. Add pasta and simmer 30 to 45 minutes. Sprinkle each serving with cheese.

cheesy turkey twists
makes 4 servings

3 cups uncooked corkscrew-shaped pasta
1 large green pepper, chopped (about 1 cup)
1 can (10¾ ounces) CAMPBELL'S® Condensed Cheddar Cheese Soup
¼ cup milk
¾ cup PACE® Picante Sauce
¼ teaspoon garlic powder or 1 clove garlic, minced
1½ cups cubed cooked turkey

1. Cook the pasta according to the package directions in a 3-quart saucepan. Add the pepper for the last 4 minutes of cooking time. Drain the pasta mixture well in a colander. Return the pasta mixture to the saucepan.

2. Stir the soup, milk, picante sauce, garlic powder and turkey in the saucepan and cook over medium heat until the mixture is hot and bubbling.

kitchen tip: You can substitute cooked chicken or 2 cans (4.5 ounces each) SWANSON® Premium Chunk White Chicken Breast, drained, for the cooked turkey.

prep time: 5 minutes • **cook time:** 20 minutes

artichoke-olive chicken bake
makes 8 servings

1½ cups uncooked rotini pasta or tri-colored rotini pasta
1 tablespoon olive oil
1 medium onion, chopped
½ green bell pepper, chopped
2 cups shredded cooked chicken
1 can (about 14 ounces) diced tomatoes with Italian herbs
1 can (14 ounces) artichoke hearts, drained and quartered
1 can (6 ounces) sliced black olives, drained
1 teaspoon Italian seasoning
2 cups (8 ounces) shredded mozzarella cheese

1. Preheat oven to 350°F. Spray 2-quart casserole with nonstick cooking spray.

2. Cook pasta according to package directions until al dente; drain.

3. Heat oil in large skillet over medium heat. Add onion and bell pepper; cook and stir 1 minute. Add pasta, chicken, tomatoes, artichokes, olives and Italian seasoning; mix until blended.

4. Place half of chicken mixture in prepared casserole; sprinkle with half of cheese. Top with remaining chicken mixture and cheese.

5. Bake, covered, 35 minutes or until hot and bubbly.

crowd pleasin' cheesy sausage ziti

makes 18 servings

1 box (16 ounces) dry ziti, cooked and drained
2 tablespoons olive oil
1 large yellow onion, chopped
2 tablespoons all-purpose flour
3 cans (12 fluid ounces *each*) NESTLÉ® CARNATION® Evaporated Milk
1½ teaspoons garlic powder
1 teaspoon salt
1 teaspoon ground black pepper
4 cups (two 8-ounce packages) shredded cheddar cheese, *divided*
4 links (12 ounces) fully-cooked chicken sausage, cut lengthwise into quarters and into ¼-inch slices
½ cup crumbled cheese snack crackers

PREHEAT oven to 375°F. Grease 13×9-inch baking dish.

HEAT oil in large saucepan over medium heat. Add onions; cook until softened. Whisk in flour; cook, stirring constantly, until mixture turns light brown, about 3 minutes. Gradually whisk in evaporated milk, garlic powder, salt and pepper; cook, stirring constantly, until sauce is thickened, about 5 minutes. Add *3½ cups cheese;* stir until melted. Add pasta and sausage; stir until thoroughly coated. Pour mixture into prepared baking dish. Sprinkle with crackers and *remaining ½ cup* cheese.

BAKE for 20 to 25 minutes or until bubbling around edges and golden brown.

cheeseburger pasta 'n vegetables dinner

makes 4 servings

1 pound ground beef
1 small onion, chopped
1 small tomato, chopped
1¾ cups water
½ cup milk
1 tablespoon I CAN'T BELIEVE IT'S NOT BUTTER!® Spread
1 package KNORR® SIDES PLUS™ Veggies - Cheddar Cheese Pasta with Broccoli & Carrots

Brown ground beef with onion in 12-inch nonstick skillet over medium-high heat; drain. Remove ground beef mixture and set aside.

Bring tomato, water, milk and Spread to a boil in same skillet over high heat. Stir in KNORR® SIDES PLUS™ Veggies - Cheddar Cheese Pasta with Broccoli & Carrots and continue boiling over medium heat, stirring occasionally, 9 minutes or until pasta is tender. Stir in ground beef mixture; heat through.

prep time: 10 minutes • **cook time:** 20 minutes

beefy pasta casserole
makes 6 servings

- 1 pound ground beef
- 1 tablespoon dried oregano leaves, crushed
- 2 cans (10¾ ounces each) CAMPBELL'S® Condensed Tomato Soup (Regular or Healthy Request®)
- 1 soup can water
- ½ of a 16-ounce package (4 cups) uncooked corkscrew-shaped pasta (rotini)
- 1 container (15 ounces) ricotta cheese
- 1 cup shredded mozzarella cheese (4 ounces)

1. Cook the beef and oregano in a 12-inch skillet over medium-high heat until the beef is well browned, stirring frequently to separate meat. Pour off any fat.

2. Stir the soup, water and pasta in a 13×9×2-inch (3-quart) shallow baking dish. Add the beef mixture and ricotta cheese and stir to coat. Cover.

3. Bake at 375°F. for 30 minutes or until hot and bubbly. Sprinkle with the mozzarella cheese. Let stand for 5 minutes or until the cheese melts.

prep time: 15 minutes • **bake time:** 30 minutes

vermont harvest mac-n-cheese

makes 5 servings

- **10 ounces elbow macaroni**
- **3 tablespoons CABOT® Salted Butter**
- **1 medium onion, finely chopped**
- **1 to 2 cloves garlic, minced**
- **1½ teaspoons minced fresh sage**
- **3 tablespoons all-purpose flour**
- **2 cups milk**
- **3 cups grated CABOT® Extra Sharp Cheddar, divided**
- **2½ cups diced smoked turkey**
- **1½ cups diced apple**
- **1½ cups croutons, lightly crushed**

1. Preheat oven to 375°F. Butter 13×9-inch baking dish.

2. In large pot of boiling salted water, cook macaroni according to package directions; drain in colander and rinse briefly under cool water. Transfer elbows to prepared baking dish and set aside.

3. In large saucepan, melt butter. Add onion, garlic and sage and cook, stirring, until onion is tender. Stir in flour and cook over low heat for several minutes until very thick.

4. Gradually stir in milk. Cook, stirring, until sauce is simmering and slightly thickened. Add 2½ cups of cheese and stir just until melted.

5. Remove sauce from heat and stir in turkey and apples.

6. Pour over reserved elbows, stirring to combine. Top with crushed croutons and remaining ½ cup cheese. Bake for 25 to 30 minutes, or until browned and bubbling.

cheeseburger macaroni

makes 4 servings

- **1 cup mostaccioli or elbow macaroni, uncooked**
- **1 pound ground beef**
- **1 medium onion, chopped**
- **1 can (14½ ounces) DEL MONTE® Diced Tomatoes with Basil, Garlic & Oregano**
- **¼ cup DEL MONTE® Tomato Ketchup**
- **1 cup (4 ounces) shredded Cheddar cheese**

1. Cook pasta according to package directions; drain.

2. Brown meat with onion in large skillet; drain. Season with salt and pepper, if desired. Stir in undrained tomatoes, ketchup and pasta; heat through.

3. Top with cheese. Garnish, if desired.

prep time: 8 minutes • **cook time:** 15 minutes

velveeta® italian sausage bake

makes 6 servings

1½ cups small penne pasta, uncooked
1 pound Italian sausage, casings removed
4 small zucchini, halved lengthwise, sliced
1 red or green bell pepper, chopped
1 can (8 ounces) pizza sauce
½ pound (8 ounces) VELVEETA® Pasteurized Prepared Cheese Product, cut into ½-inch cubes
1½ cups KRAFT® 100% Grated Parmesan Cheese

1. HEAT oven to 350°F. Cook pasta as directed on package. Meanwhile, brown sausage in large deep skillet on medium-high heat, stirring occasionally to break up the sausage. Drain; return sausage to skillet. Add zucchini, pepper and pizza sauce; stir until well blended. Cook 5 to 6 minutes or until vegetables are tender, stirring occasionally. Drain pasta. Add to sausage mixture along with the VELVEETA®; stir until well blended.

2. SPOON into 13×9-inch baking dish sprayed with cooking spray; sprinkle with Parmesan.

3. BAKE 15 to 20 minutes or until heated through.

prep time: 25 minutes • **total time:** 45 minutes

kid friendly: Prepare as directed, substituting 1 pound lean ground beef for the sausage and 1 cup each shredded carrots and zucchini for the 4 sliced zucchini. Also, try using a fun pasta shape, such as wagon wheels.

velveeta® sausage and rice casserole: Omit pasta. Prepare as directed, adding 1½ cups uncooked instant white rice and 1½ cups water to the meat mixture along with the VELVEETA. Increase the baking time to 35 to 40 minutes or until rice is tender and casserole is heated through. Makes 8 servings.

veggie versions

spicy macaroni and cheese with broccoli

makes 2 servings

    1 tablespoon all-purpose flour
    1 cup evaporated milk, divided
    1 teaspoon Dijon mustard
    ¼ teaspoon dried thyme
    ¼ teaspoon salt
    ¼ teaspoon black pepper
    ⅛ to ¼ teaspoon red pepper flakes
    ½ cup (2 ounces) shredded sharp Cheddar cheese
    2 cups small broccoli florets, blanched*
    1⅓ cups cooked whole grain macaroni
    ¼ cup crushed baked tortilla chips

Bring water to a boil in medium saucepan over high heat. Cook broccoli in boiling water about 1 minute. Remove from saucepan and plunge into cold water.

1. Preheat oven to 350°F. Spray 1-quart baking dish with nonstick cooking spray.

2. Stir flour into ¼ cup milk in small saucepan until smooth paste forms. Gradually add remaining ¾ cup milk, mustard, thyme, salt, black pepper and red pepper flakes. Cook over low heat, stirring constantly until mixture slightly thickens. Gradually add cheese, stirring until melted. Remove from heat. Stir in broccoli and macaroni.

3. Spoon mixture into prepared baking dish. Sprinkle tortilla chips on top. Bake 25 minutes or until bubbly and slightly browned. Let stand 5 minutes before serving.

turkey veggie tetrazzini
makes 12 servings

8 ounces dry whole wheat spaghetti
1 package (16 ounces) frozen Italian-style vegetable blend (broccoli, red peppers, mushrooms and onions)
1 tablespoon olive oil
¼ cup all-purpose flour
½ teaspoon garlic powder
¼ teaspoon salt
¼ teaspoon ground black pepper
1 can (14.5 fluid ounces) reduced sodium chicken broth
1 can (12 fluid ounces) NESTLÉ® CARNATION® Evaporated Lowfat 2% Milk
¾ cup (2.25 ounces) shredded Parmesan cheese, *divided*
2 cups cooked, chopped turkey breast meat

PREHEAT oven to 350°F. Lightly grease 13×9-inch baking dish.

PREPARE pasta according to package directions, adding frozen vegetables to boiling pasta water for last minute of cooking time; drain. Return pasta and vegetables to cooking pot.

MEANWHILE heat oil in medium saucepan over medium heat. Stir in flour, garlic powder, salt and pepper; cook, stirring constantly, for 1 minute. Remove from heat; gradually stir in broth. Return to heat; bring to boil over medium heat, stirring constantly. Stir in evaporated milk and ½ cup cheese; cook over low heat until cheese melts. Remove from heat. Stir in turkey.

POUR cheese sauce over pasta and vegetables; mix lightly. Pour into prepared baking dish. Sprinkle with *remaining ¼ cup* cheese.

BAKE for 20 to 25 minutes or until lightly browned. Serve immediately.

tuna tomato casserole
makes 6 servings

  1 package (12 ounces) wide egg noodles
  2 cans (6 ounces each) tuna, drained and
      flaked
  1 cup mayonnaise
  1 onion, finely chopped
  ¼ teaspoon salt
  ¼ teaspoon black pepper
  8 to 10 plum tomatoes, sliced ¼ inch thick
  1 cup (4 ounces) shredded Cheddar or mozzarella cheese

1. Preheat oven to 375°F. Cook noodles according to package directions. Drain and return to saucepan.

2. Combine tuna, mayonnaise, onion, salt and pepper in medium bowl; mix well. Stir tuna mixture into noodles until well blended.

3. Layer half of noodle mixture, half of tomatoes and half of cheese in 13×9-inch baking dish. Press down slightly. Repeat layers.

4. Bake 20 minutes or until cheese is melted and casserole is heated through.

broccoli & cheese stuffed shells
makes 6 servings

1 container (15 ounces) ricotta cheese

1 package (10 ounces) frozen chopped broccoli, thawed and well drained

1 cup shredded mozzarella cheese (about 4 ounces)

⅓ cup grated Parmesan cheese

¼ teaspoon black pepper

18 jumbo shell-shaped pasta, cooked and drained

1 jar (24 ounces) PREGO® Chunky Garden Combination Italian Sauce

1. Stir the ricotta cheese, broccoli, ½ **cup** of the mozzarella cheese, Parmesan cheese and black pepper in a medium bowl. Spoon **about 2 tablespoons** of the cheese mixture into **each** shell.

2. Spread **1 cup** of the Italian sauce in a 13×9×2-inch shallow baking dish. Place the filled shells on the sauce. Pour the remaining sauce over the shells. Sprinkle with the remaining mozzarella cheese.

3. Bake at 400°F. for 25 minutes or until it's hot and bubbling.

kitchen tip: To save time, thaw the broccoli in the microwave on HIGH for 4 minutes.

prep time: 25 minutes • **bake time:** 25 minutes

creamy chicken and pasta with spinach

makes 8 servings

- **6 ounces uncooked egg noodles**
- **1 tablespoon olive oil**
- **¼ cup chopped onion**
- **¼ cup chopped red bell pepper**
- **1 package (10 ounces) frozen spinach, thawed and drained**
- **2 boneless skinless chicken breasts (¾ pound), cooked and cut into 1-inch pieces**
- **1 can (4 ounces) sliced mushrooms, drained**
- **2 cups (8 ounces) shredded Swiss cheese**
- **1 container (8 ounces) sour cream**
- **¾ cup half-and-half**
- **2 eggs, lightly beaten**
- **½ teaspoon salt**

1. Preheat oven to 350°F. Cook noodles according to package directions; drain and set aside. Spray 13×9-inch baking dish with nonstick cooking spray.

2. Heat oil in large skillet over medium-high heat. Add onion and bell pepper; cook and stir 2 minutes or until onion is tender. Add spinach, chicken, mushrooms and cooked noodles; stir to blend.

3. Combine cheese, sour cream, half-and-half, eggs and salt in medium bowl; blend well.

4. Add cheese mixture to chicken mixture; stir to blend. Transfer to prepared baking dish. Bake, covered, 30 to 35 minutes or until heated through.

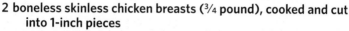

easy pumpkin-pasta bake
makes 10 servings

Nonstick cooking spray
1 pound (about 4 links) sweet or spicy
  lean Italian turkey sausage, casings
  removed
1 tablespoon finely chopped garlic
1 jar (24 to 26 ounces) marinara sauce
½ cup water or dry red or white wine
1 can (15 ounces) LIBBY'S® 100% Pure
  Pumpkin
4 tablespoons (0.75 ounce) shredded Parmesan cheese, *divided*
1 box (14.5 ounces) whole wheat penne or other short-cut
  pasta, prepared according to package directions
1 cup (4 ounces) shredded low-moisture part-skim mozzarella
  cheese

PREHEAT oven to 375°F. Spray 3-quart casserole dish or 13×9-inch
baking dish with nonstick cooking spray.

COOK sausage in large skillet over medium-high heat until cooked
through. Stir in garlic; cook for 1 minute. Stir in marinara sauce
(reserve jar). Add water or wine to jar; cover and shake. Pour into
skillet along with pumpkin and *2 tablespoons* Parmesan cheese. Stir
well. Stir in prepared pasta. Spoon into prepared dish. Sprinkle with
remaining 2 tablespoons Parmesan cheese and mozzarella cheese;
cover.

BAKE for 15 minutes. Carefully remove cover; bake for an additional
5 minutes or until cheese is melted and bubbly.

cheesy spinach bake
makes 6 servings

 8 ounces uncooked spinach fettuccine noodles
 1 tablespoon vegetable oil
1½ cups sliced fresh mushrooms
 2 green onions, finely chopped
 1 teaspoon garlic
 1 package (10 ounces) frozen spinach, thawed and drained
 2 tablespoons water
 1 container (15 ounces) ricotta cheese
¾ cup whipping cream
 1 egg
½ teaspoon ground nutmeg
½ teaspoon black pepper
½ cup (2 ounces) shredded Swiss cheese

1. Preheat oven to 350°F. Spray 1½-quart casserole with nonstick cooking spray. Cook pasta according to package directions; drain.

2. Heat oil in medium skillet over medium heat. Add mushrooms, green onions and garlic. Cook and stir until mushrooms are softened. Add spinach and water. Cover; cook 3 minutes or until spinach is wilted.

3. Combine ricotta cheese, cream, egg, nutmeg and black pepper in large bowl. Gently stir in noodles and vegetables; toss to coat evenly. Spread noodle mixture in prepared casserole. Sprinkle with Swiss cheese.

4. Bake 25 to 30 minutes or until heated through.

penne with sausage and feta

makes 6 servings

    6 ounces uncooked penne or rigatoni pasta
      Nonstick cooking spray
   12 ounces mild Italian bulk sausage*
   ¼ teaspoon red pepper flakes
    2 cups packed baby spinach leaves or
      spring greens
   ½ cup roasted red peppers, cut into thin strips
   24 pitted kalamata olives, coarsely chopped
   ¼ cup chopped fresh basil
    2 tablespoons extra virgin olive oil
    1 cup (4 ounces) crumbled feta cheese with tomatoes and basil
   ¼ teaspoon salt

*If bulk sausage is not available, purchase regular sausage links and remove casings before cooking.

1. Cook pasta according to package directions. Drain well; cover and keep warm.

2. Meanwhile, coat large skillet with cooking spray; heat over medium-high heat. Add sausage and pepper flakes. Cook 5 minutes until sausage is cooked through, stirring to break up meat. Drain fat.

3. Add pasta, spinach, roasted peppers, olives, basil and oil to sausage mixture. Gently toss until spinach has wilted slightly. Stir in feta and salt.

garden vegetable lasagna
makes 8 servings

- 1 container (15 ounces) ricotta cheese
- 8 ounces shredded mozzarella cheese (about 2 cups)
- 2 eggs
- 4 medium carrots, shredded (about 2 cups)
- 1 package (10 ounces) frozen chopped broccoli, thawed and well drained
- 9 lasagna noodles, cooked and drained
- 1 jar (24 ounces) PREGO® Chunky Garden Combination Italian Sauce
- Grated Parmesan cheese

1. Mix ricotta cheese, **1 cup** mozzarella cheese, eggs, carrots and broccoli in a medium bowl and set it aside.

2. Place **3** lasagna noodles in greased 3-quart shallow baking dish. Top with **half** of the vegetable mixture and **1 cup** of the Italian sauce. Repeat the layers. Top with the remaining lasagna noodles and remaining sauce. Sprinkle with the remaining mozzarella cheese.

3. Bake at 400°F. for 30 minutes or until it's hot and bubbling. Let stand for 10 minutes. Serve with the Parmesan cheese.

kitchen tip: To thaw the broccoli, microwave on for HIGH 4 minutes.

prep time: 25 minutes • **cook time:** 40 minutes

chicken-asparagus casserole

makes 12 servings

- 2 teaspoons vegetable oil
- 1 cup chopped green and/or red bell peppers
- 1 medium onion, chopped
- 2 cloves garlic, minced
- 1 can (10¾ ounces) condensed cream of asparagus soup, undiluted
- 1 container (8 ounces) ricotta cheese
- 2 cups (8 ounces) shredded Cheddar cheese, divided
- 2 eggs
- 1½ cups chopped cooked chicken
- 1 package (10 ounces) frozen chopped asparagus,* thawed and drained
- 8 ounces egg noodles, cooked
- Black pepper (optional)

*Or, substitute ½ pound fresh asparagus cut into ½-inch pieces. Bring 6 cups water to a boil over high heat in large saucepan. Add asparagus; cook 3 to 4 minutes or until crisp-tender. Drain.

1. Preheat oven to 350°F. Grease 13×9-inch casserole.

2. Heat oil in small skillet over medium heat. Add bell peppers, onion and garlic; cook and stir until vegetables are crisp-tender.

3. Mix soup, ricotta cheese, 1 cup Cheddar cheese and eggs in large bowl until well blended. Add onion mixture, chicken, asparagus and noodles; mix well. Season with pepper, if desired.

4. Spread mixture evenly in prepared casserole. Top with remaining 1 cup Cheddar cheese.

5. Bake 30 minutes or until center is set and cheese is bubbly. Let stand 5 minutes before serving.

zucchini and mushroom lasagna with tofu

makes 4 to 6 servings

1 tablespoon olive oil
1 cup chopped onions
1 package (8 ounces) sliced mushrooms
2 small zucchini, thinly sliced
½ teaspoon black pepper, divided
½ (14-ounce) package tofu
1 egg
¼ teaspoon salt
1 jar (26 ounces) spicy red pepper pasta sauce
9 uncooked no-boil lasagna noodles
2 cups (8 ounces) shredded Italian cheese blend
¼ cup shredded Parmesan cheese

1. Preheat oven to 350°F. Spray 9-inch square baking dish with nonstick cooking spray.

2 . Heat oil in large skillet. Add onions; cook and stir 2 minutes. Add mushrooms, zucchini and ¼ teaspoon pepper. Cook and stir 8 minutes or until softened.

3. Meanwhile, combine tofu, egg, salt and remaining ¼ teaspoon pepper in medium bowl. Mix until smooth; set aside.

4. Spread ½ cup pasta sauce in bottom of prepared dish. Arrange 3 noodles over sauce. Layer one third of vegetable mixture, tofu mixture, pasta sauce and Italian cheese blend. Repeat layers twice. Cover with foil.

5. Bake 1 hour. Remove foil; sprinkle with Parmesan cheese. Bake, uncovered, 15 minutes or until cheese is browned. Let stand 15 minutes before serving.

old-fashioned macaroni & cheese with broccoli

makes 4 servings

2 cups (8 ounces) uncooked elbow macaroni
3 cups small broccoli florets
1 tablespoon butter
1 tablespoon all-purpose flour
½ teaspoon salt
⅛ teaspoon black pepper
1¾ cups milk
1½ cups (6 ounces) shredded sharp Cheddar cheese

1. Cook pasta according to package directions. Add broccoli during last 5 minutes of cooking time. Drain pasta and broccoli; return to pan.

2. Meanwhile, melt butter in small saucepan over medium heat. Add flour, salt and pepper; cook and stir 1 minute until smooth paste forms. Stir in milk; bring to a boil over medium-high heat, stirring frequently. Reduce heat and simmer 2 minutes or until thickened. Remove from heat. Gradually stir in cheese until melted.

3. Add sauce to pasta and broccoli; stir until blended.

macaroni-stuffed peppers

makes 6 servings

> **3** green bell peppers, halved lengthwise, cored
> **2** tablespoons unsalted butter
> **½** cup finely chopped red bell pepper
> **2** tablespoons all-purpose flour
> **2** cups milk, heated
> **1¾** cups (7 ounces) shredded sharp Cheddar cheese, divided
> **½** teaspoon salt
> **½** teaspoon paprika
> **¼** teaspoon pepper
> **2** cups cooked macaroni (about 1 cup uncooked)
> **¼** cup coarse dry bread crumbs (panko)

1. Preheat oven to 350°F. Spray 13×9-inch baking dish with nonstick cooking spray.

2. Bring large saucepan of water to a boil. Add pepper halves, press under water and boil 2 minutes. Remove; drain well.

3. Melt butter in large saucepan. Add red bell pepper and cook over medium heat 5 minutes, stirring frequently. Stir in flour until smooth paste forms. Gradually whisk in milk. Cook 4 to 5 minutes, whisking constantly, until mixture begins to thicken. Gradually stir in 1½ cups Cheddar cheese, stirring until melted. Season with salt, paprika and pepper. Stir in macaroni.

4. Arrange pepper halves, cut-sides up in baking dish. Spoon ¾ cup macaroni mixture into each pepper half. Combine remaining ¼ cup cheese with bread crumbs. Sprinkle on top.

5. Bake 20 to 25 minutes or until lightly browned and peppers are tender.

tofu rigatoni casserole
makes 6 servings

- **3 cups uncooked rigatoni**
- **4 cups loosely packed baby spinach**
- **1 cup soft tofu**
- **1 egg**
- **¼ teaspoon salt**
- **¼ teaspoon black pepper**
- **¼ teaspoon ground nutmeg (optional)**
- **1 can (about 14 ounces) diced tomatoes with basil, garlic and oregano**
- **1 can (about 14 ounces) quartered artichokes, drained and chopped**
- **2 cups (8 ounces) shredded Italian cheese blend, divided**

1. Preheat oven to 350°F. Spray 11×7-inch baking dish with nonstick cooking spray.

2. Cook rigatoni in large saucepan according to package directions. Stir in spinach in bunches during last 2 minutes of cooking just until wilted. Drain; return to saucepan.

3. Meanwhile, combine tofu, egg, salt, pepper and nutmeg, if desired, in medium bowl; mix until blended. Fold tofu mixture into rigatoni. Add tomatoes, artichokes and 1½ cups cheese; mix well. Spoon into prepared baking dish.

4. Bake 20 minutes. Top with remaining ½ cup cheese. Bake 10 minutes or until cheese is browned.

tip: If the saucepan is too small to cook the spinach with the pasta, chop the spinach and stir it in with the tomatoes.

crab-artichoke casserole
makes 6 servings

   8 ounces uncooked small shell pasta
   2 tablespoons butter
   6 green onions, chopped
   2 tablespoons all-purpose flour
   1 cup half-and-half
   1 teaspoon dry mustard
 ½ teaspoon ground red pepper
   Salt and black pepper
 ½ cup (2 ounces) shredded Swiss cheese, divided
   1 package (about 8 ounces) imitation crabmeat
   1 can (about 14 ounces) artichoke hearts, drained and cut into
      bite-size pieces

1. Preheat oven to 350°F. Grease 2-quart casserole. Cook pasta according to package directions; drain and set aside.

2. Melt butter in large saucepan over medium heat. Add green onions; cook and stir about 2 minutes. Add flour; cook and stir 2 minutes. Gradually add half-and-half, whisking constantly until mixture begins to thicken. Whisk in mustard and red pepper; season to taste with salt and black pepper. Remove from heat; stir in ¼ cup cheese until melted.

3. Combine crabmeat, artichokes and pasta in prepared casserole. Add sauce mixture; stir until blended. Top with remaining ¼ cup cheese. Bake about 40 minutes or until hot, bubbly and lightly browned.

tip: This can also be baked in individual ovenproof dishes. Reduce baking time to about 20 minutes.

kale, gorgonzola & noodle casserole
makes 6 servings

- 1 large bunch kale, stemmed and coarsely chopped (about 8 cups chopped)
- 2 tablespoons unsalted butter
- 1 small garlic clove, smashed
- ¼ cup chopped green onions
- 2 tablespoons all-purpose flour
- 4 ounces Gorgonzola cheese, crumbled
- 4 ounces fontina cheese, cut into small pieces
- ½ teaspoon salt
- ¼ teaspoon pepper
- ¼ teaspoon ground nutmeg
- 6 ounces egg noodles or fettuccine, cooked (about 3½ to 4 cups uncooked)
- ¼ cup coarse dry bread crumbs (panko)

1. Preheat oven to 350°F. Spray 9-inch square baking dish with nonstick cooking spray.

2. Place kale in large saucepan with 1 inch water. Cover; bring to a simmer. Steam kale 15 minutes or until tender. Drain well, pressing out excess liquid; set aside.

3. Melt butter in large saucepan or deep skillet over medium-low heat. Add garlic and green onions; cook and stir over low heat 5 minutes. Discard garlic. Whisk in flour until smooth paste forms. Cook and stir 2 minutes without browning. Gradually add half-and-half, stirring frequently, until mixture thickens. Gradually add cheese until melted. Stir in salt, pepper and nutmeg. Stir in noodles and kale; mix well.

4. Spoon into prepared baking dish. Sprinkle with bread crumbs. Bake 30 minutes or until bubbly. If desired, place dish until broiler for 30 seconds to brown.

broccoli mac & cheese
makes 6 servings

- **2 cups elbow macaroni**
- **¼ cup butter**
- **¼ cup all-purpose flour**
- **2 cups milk**
- **2 cups (8 ounces) SARGENTO® Shredded Sharp Cheddar Cheese**
- **½ cup chopped onion**
- **2 cups (16 ounces) broccoli florets, steamed**
- **2 English muffins, cut into ½-inch pieces**

PREHEAT oven to 350°F. Prepare macaroni according to package directions.

MEANWHILE, melt butter in large saucepan over medium heat. Stir in flour until smooth; cook and stir 2 minutes. Gradually add milk, stirring constantly, until mixture is slightly thickened.

ADD cheese and onion. Cook, stirring constantly, until cheese melts. Add broccoli and macaroni; stir well.

PLACE in 3-quart casserole. Sprinkle English muffin pieces evenly over top. Bake 15 to 20 minutes or until muffin pieces are golden brown.

prep time: 10 minutes • **cook time:** 30 minutes

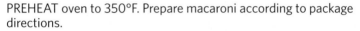

baked pasta primavera casserole

makes 6 servings

1 jar (1 pound 10 ounces) RAGÚ® Old World Style® Pasta Sauce

1 cup shredded part-skim mozzarella cheese (about 4 ounces)

1 bag (16 ounces) frozen Italian-style vegetables, thawed

1 box (16 ounces) ziti or penne pasta, cooked and drained

¼ cup grated Parmesan cheese

1. Preheat oven to 350°F. Combine Pasta Sauce, ½ cup mozzarella cheese and Parmesan cheese in large bowl. Stir in vegetables and hot ziti.

2. Spoon pasta mixture into 2½-quart casserole; sprinkle with remaining ½ cup mozzarella cheese.

3. Bake, uncovered, 30 minutes or until heated through. Sprinkle with Parmesan cheese.

prep time: 20 minutes • **cook time:** 30 minutes

ethnic twists

shells & fontina
makes 4 servings

      8 ounces small shell whole wheat pasta
  1¾ cups milk
      4 large fresh sage leaves (optional)
      3 tablespoons butter
  ¼ cup all-purpose flour
  ½ cup tomato sauce
      Salt and black pepper
  ¾ cup grated Parmesan cheese, divided
  5½ ounces fontina cheese
  ¼ cup dry bread crumbs

1. Preheat oven to 350°F. Cook pasta according to package directions until barely al dente. Run under cold water to stop cooking; drain.

2. Meanwhile, heat milk with sage leaves, if desired, in small saucepan over medium heat; do not boil. Melt butter in large saucepan or deep skillet over medium-low heat until bubbly. Whisk in flour until smooth paste forms; cook and stir 2 minutes without browning. Remove sage and gradually whisk in milk over medium heat; cook 6 to 8 minutes, whisking constantly until mixture begins to bubble and thickens slightly. Stir in tomato sauce and season with salt and pepper. Remove from heat; stir in ½ cup Parmesan cheese until smooth.

3. Combine pasta and sauce. Coarsely shred fontina cheese.* Transfer one third of pasta mixture to 2-quart casserole. Top with one third of shredded fontina. Repeat layers twice. Sprinkle with bread crumbs.

4. Bake 20 to 25 minutes or until hot and bubbly.

It is easier to shred fontina cheese if it is very cold. Keep it in the refrigerator, or place it in the freezer for 10 minutes before shredding.

pasta with onions and goat cheese
makes 4 servings

2 teaspoons olive oil
3 to 4 cups thinly sliced sweet onions
¾ cup (3 ounces) crumbled goat cheese
¼ cup milk
6 ounces uncooked baby bowtie or other small pasta
1 clove garlic, minced
2 tablespoons dry white wine or vegetable broth
1½ teaspoons chopped fresh sage *or* ½ teaspoon dried sage
½ teaspoon salt
¼ teaspoon black pepper
2 tablespoons chopped toasted walnuts

1. Heat oil in large nonstick skillet over medium heat. Add onions; cook slowly until golden and caramelized, about 20 to 25 minutes, stirring occasionally.

2. Combine goat cheese and milk in small bowl; stir until well blended. Set aside.

3. Cook pasta according to package directions. Drain and set aside.

4. Add garlic to onions in skillet; cook about 3 minutes or until softened. Add wine, sage, salt and pepper; cook until liquid has evaporated. Remove from heat. Add pasta and goat cheese mixture; stir until cheese is melted. Sprinkle with walnuts.

italian mac & cheese
makes 6 servings

2 tablespoons butter
2 tablespoons all-purpose flour
2½ cups milk
¾ teaspoon salt
¼ teaspoon crushed red pepper flakes or black pepper
2 cups (8 ounces) SARGENTO® BISTRO® Blends Shredded Italian Pasta Cheese, divided
8 ounces multi-grain elbow macaroni (2 cups dry), cooked and drained
1 cup Italian or sourdough fresh bread crumbs
1 tablespoon olive oil

MELT butter in a large saucepan over medium heat. Add flour; cook and stir 1 minute. Add milk, salt and pepper flakes. Bring to a boil, stirring frequently. Reduce heat; simmer 2 minutes or until sauce thickens. Stir in 1½ cups cheese until melted. Stir in cooked macaroni; immediately transfer mixture to a greased or sprayed 8- or 9-inch baking dish.

TOSS bread crumbs with oil and remaining cheese; sprinkle over mac and cheese mixture. Bake in a preheated 375°F oven 20 to 25 minutes or until heated through and topping is golden brown.

prep time: 20 minutes • **cook time:** 25 minutes

reuben noodle bake

makes 6 servings

8 ounces uncooked egg noodles
5 ounces thinly sliced deli-style corned beef
2 cups (8 ounces) shredded Swiss cheese
1 can (about 14 ounces) sauerkraut with caraway seeds, drained
½ cup Thousand Island dressing
½ cup milk
1 tablespoon mustard
2 slices pumpernickel bread
1 tablespoon butter, melted

1. Preheat oven to 350°F. Spray 13×9-inch baking dish with nonstick cooking spray. Cook noodles according to package directions until almost tender. Drain.

2. Meanwhile, cut corned beef into bite-size pieces. Combine noodles, corned beef, cheese and sauerkraut in large bowl. Transfer to prepared baking dish.

3. Combine dressing, milk and mustard in small bowl. Spoon evenly over noodle mixture.

4. Tear bread into large pieces; process in food processor or blender until crumbs form. Combine bread crumbs and butter in small bowl; sprinkle evenly over casserole. Bake 25 to 30 minutes or until heated through.

cheesy italian pasta bake
makes 6 servings

1½ cups wagon wheel pasta, uncooked
1 pound extra lean ground beef
1 large carrot, shredded (about 1 cup)
1 large zucchini, shredded (about 1 cup)
1 red pepper, chopped
1 can (8 ounces) pizza sauce
½ pound (8 ounces) VELVEETA® 2% Milk Pasteurized Prepared Cheese Product, cut into ½-inch cubes
½ cup KRAFT® Grated Parmesan Cheese

1. HEAT oven to 350°F. Cook pasta as directed on package. Meanwhile, brown meat in large nonstick skillet on medium-high heat; drain. Stir in vegetables and sauce; cook 5 minutes or until vegetables are tender. Drain pasta. Add to meat mixture along with VELVEETA®; mix well.

2. SPOON into 8-inch square baking dish sprayed with cooking spray; sprinkle with Parmesan.

3. BAKE 15 to 20 minutes or until heated through.

tip: Save 50 calories and 6 grams of fat, including 3 grams of saturated fat per serving by preparing with whole wheat pasta, extra lean ground beef and VELVEETA® 2% Milk Pasteurized Prepared Cheese Product.

substitute: Prepare using any other bite-size pasta.

prep time: 25 minutes • **total time:** 45 minutes

south-of-the-border macaroni & cheese

makes 4 servings

- 5 cups cooked rotini pasta
- 2 cups (8 ounces) cubed American cheese
- 1 can (12 ounces) evaporated milk
- 1 cup (4 ounces) cubed sharp Cheddar cheese
- 1 can (4 ounces) diced green chiles, drained
- 2 teaspoons chili powder
- 2 medium tomatoes, seeded and chopped
- 5 green onions, sliced

slow cooker directions

1. Combine pasta, American cheese, evaporated milk, Cheddar cheese, chiles and chili powder in slow cooker; mix well. Cover; cook on HIGH 2 hours, stirring occasionally.

2. Stir in tomatoes and green onions; continue cooking until heated through.

tip: Serve this easy main dish with Mexican-inspired sides. Start with chips and fresh salsa. A tomato-avocado salad would go well, and for dessert, offer mango ice cream.

chicken & broccoli alfredo
makes 4 servings

½ **of a 16-ounce package linguine**
1 **cup fresh or frozen broccoli flowerets**
2 **tablespoons butter**
4 **skinless, boneless chicken breast halves (about 1 pound), cut into 1½-inch pieces**
1 **can (10¾ ounces) CAMPBELL'S® Condensed Cream of Mushroom Soup (Regular, 98% Fat Free or Healthy Request®)**
½ **cup milk**
½ **cup grated Parmesan cheese**
¼ **teaspoon ground black pepper**

1. Prepare the linguine according to the package directions in a 3-quart saucepan. Add the broccoli during the last 4 minutes of the cooking time. Drain the linguine mixture well in a colander.

2. Heat the butter in a 10-inch skillet over medium-high heat. Add the chicken and cook until it's well browned, stirring often.

3. Stir the soup, milk, cheese, black pepper and linguine mixture in the skillet and cook until the chicken is cooked through, stirring occasionally. Serve with additional Parmesan cheese.

grilled chicken & broccoli alfredo: Substitute grilled chicken breasts for the skinless, boneless chicken.

shrimp & broccoli alfredo: Substitute 1 pound fresh extra large shrimp, shelled and deveined, for the chicken. Cook as directed for the chicken, until the shrimp are cooked through.

serving suggestion: Serve with a mixed green salad topped with orange sections, walnut pieces and raspberry vinaigrette. For dessert serve almond biscotti.

prep time: 10 minutes • **cook time:** 20 minutes

now & later baked ziti
makes 12 servings

2 pounds ground beef
1 large onion, chopped (about 1 cup)
7½ cups PREGO® Fresh Mushroom Italian Sauce
9 cups tube-shaped pasta (ziti), cooked and drained
12 ounces shredded mozzarella cheese (about 3 cups)
½ cup grated Parmesan cheese

1. Cook the beef and onion in an 8-quart saucepot over medium high heat until the beef is well browned, stirring often to separate the meat. Pour off any fat.

2. Stir the sauce, ziti and **2 cups** mozzarella cheese in the saucepot. Spoon the beef mixture into **2** (12½×8½×2-inch) disposable foil pans. Top with the remaining mozzarella and Parmesan cheeses.

3. Bake at 350°F. for 30 minutes or until the beef mixture is hot and the cheese is melted.

kitchen tip: To make ahead and freeze, prepare the ziti as directed above but do not bake. Cover the pans with foil and freeze. Bake the frozen ziti, uncovered, at 350°F. for 1 hour or until it's hot. Or, thaw the ziti in the refrigerator for 24 hours, then bake, uncovered, at 350°F. for 45 minutes or until it's hot.

serving suggestion: Serve with zucchini cut into thinly sliced ribbons (use vegetable peeler) and sautéed in olive oil. Sprinkle with grated Parmesan. For dessert serve lemon sorbet with a mint sprig.

prep time: 15 minutes • **cook time:** 30 minutes

tomato, brie & noodle casserole
makes 6 servings

- 1 pint grape tomatoes, halved lengthwise
- 2 teaspoons vegetable oil
- ¾ teaspoon salt, divided
- 2 tablespoons butter
- 1 clove garlic
- 2 tablespoons all-purpose flour
- 2 cups half-and-half, heated
- 8 ounces good-quality ripe Brie, crust removed, cut into small chunks
- ¼ cup finely chopped fresh basil
- 2 tablespoons minced fresh chives
- ¼ teaspoon pepper
- 6 ounces egg noodles, cooked
- ¼ cup sliced almonds

1. Preheat oven to 425°F. Line baking sheet with heavy-duty aluminum foil. Spray 9-inch square baking dish with nonstick cooking spray.

2. Spread tomatoes on prepared baking sheet. Sprinkle with oil and ¼ teaspoon salt. Roast 20 minutes or until tender and slightly shriveled; set aside. Reduce oven temperature to 350°F.

3. Melt butter in large saucepan or deep skillet over medium heat. Add garlic clove and cook 1 minute. Stir in flour until smooth paste forms; cook 2 minutes without browning. Gradually add half-and-half, stirring until thickened. Remove and discard garlic. Gradually stir in cheese until melted.

4. Add basil, chives, remaining ½ teaspoon salt and pepper. Stir in noodles. Drain off any liquid from tomatoes; fold into noodle mixture. Spread in prepared baking dish.

5. Bake 17 to 20 minutes or until sauce starts to bubble. Sprinkle with almonds; bake 8 to 10 minutes or until nuts turn light golden brown.

italian three-cheese macaroni

makes 4 servings

2 cups uncooked elbow macaroni
¼ cup (½ stick) butter
3 tablespoons all-purpose flour
1 teaspoon Italian seasoning
½ to 1 teaspoon black pepper
½ teaspoon salt
2 cups milk
¾ cup (3 ounces) shredded Cheddar cheese
¼ cup grated Parmesan cheese
1 can (about 14 ounces) diced tomatoes, drained
1 cup (4 ounces) shredded mozzarella cheese
½ cup dry bread crumbs

1. Preheat oven to 350°F. Spray 2-quart casserole with nonstick cooking spray.

2. Cook macaroni according to package directions until al dente. Drain and set aside.

3. Melt butter in medium saucepan over medium heat. Whisk in flour, Italian seasoning, pepper and salt, stirring until smooth paste forms; cook 2 minutes without browning. Gradually add milk, whisking constantly until slightly thickened. Add Cheddar and Parmesan; stir until smooth.

4. Layer half of pasta, half of tomatoes and half of cheese sauce in prepared dish. Repeat layers.

5. Sprinkle mozzarella and bread crumbs evenly over casserole.

6. Bake, covered, 30 minutes or until heated through. Uncover and bake 5 minutes or until bubbly and golden brown.

classic chicken tetrazzini
makes 6 servings

> **2 cans (12.5 ounces each) TYSON® Premium Chunk Chicken Breast**
> **2 bags (8 ounces each) extra-wide egg noodles**
> **2 cans (10 ounces each) condensed cream of mushroom soup**
> **1½ cups (6 ounces) shredded cheese, divided**
> **2 tablespoons chopped pimentos**

1. Preheat oven to 375°F. Bring 6 cups water and broth from both cans of chicken to a boil in large pot. Add noodles and cook until tender; drain well.

2. Mix together noodles, soup, chicken, ¾ cup cheese and pimentos. Place in 13×9-inch casserole dish. Bake 15 minutes. Top with remaining cheese and bake until cheese is melted. Refrigerate leftovers immediately.

serving suggestion: Serve with choice of vegetable and bread.

tip: This recipe provides a great way to use up leftover chicken.

cook time: 30 minutes

greek skillet linguine
makes 4 servings

- ½ **pound uncooked linguine**
- ½ **(3-ounce) package sun-dried tomatoes (not packed in oil)**
- 1 **cup boiling water**
- 3 **tablespoons extra virgin olive oil, divided**
- ½ **cup chopped onion**
- 4 **cloves garlic, minced**
- 1½ **pounds raw large shrimp, peeled and deveined**
- 1¼ **teaspoons dried oregano**
- ½ **teaspoon salt**
- 2 **cans artichoke hearts, well drained and quartered**
- 14 **kalamata or black olives, pitted and coarsely chopped**
- 2 **tablespoons balsamic vinegar**
- ½ **cup crumbled feta cheese**

1. Cook pasta according to package directions; drain.

2. Meanwhile, place tomatoes in small bowl. Add 1 cup boiling water; let stand 10 minutes. Drain well and chop.

3. Heat 1 tablespoon oil in large skillet over medium-high heat 1 minute. Add onion and garlic; cook and stir 3 minutes. Add shrimp, oregano and salt; cook 4 to 5 minutes or until shrimp are opaque, stirring frequently. Add artichoke hearts, olives and reserved tomatoes. Stir gently; cook 3 minutes.

4. Remove skillet from heat. Gently stir in vinegar and remaining 2 tablespoons oil. Cover; let stand 5 minutes. Serve shrimp mixture over pasta and sprinkle with cheese.

catalonian stew

makes 6 servings

- 2 boneless skinless chicken breasts, cut into bite-size pieces
- 3 ounces pepperoni, diced
- 1 tablespoon vegetable oil
- 2 cans (15 ounces each) tomato sauce
- 3 cups chicken broth
- 1 cup pimiento-stuffed green olives, halved
- 2 tablespoons sugar
- 8 ounces uncooked rotini or other shaped pasta
- ⅓ cup chopped fresh parsley
- ⅛ teaspoon crushed saffron, optional
- 1 cup (4 ounces) SARGENTO® Fancy Shredded Mild or Sharp Cheddar Cheese
- 1 cup (4 ounces) SARGENTO® Fancy Shredded Monterey Jack Cheese

In Dutch oven, cook chicken and pepperoni in oil over medium heat until chicken is lightly browned, about 5 minutes; drain. Add tomato sauce, chicken broth, olives and sugar. Bring to a boil; reduce heat and simmer, covered, 15 minutes. Return to a boil. Add rotini, parsley and saffron, if desired; cover and cook an additional 15 minutes or until pasta is tender. Combine Cheddar and Monterey Jack cheeses in small bowl. Spoon stew into 6 individual ovenproof serving bowls; sprinkle evenly with cheese. Bake in preheated 350°F oven about 5 minutes or until cheese is melted.

italian-style mac & cheese with chicken sausage

makes 6 servings

- 2 cups (8 ounces) dry elbow macaroni (regular or whole wheat)
- 1 can (12 fluid ounces) NESTLÉ® CARNATION® Evaporated Lowfat 2% Milk
- 2 cups (8-ounce package) shredded Italian-style 4- or 5-cheese blend
- 2 links (6 ounces) fully cooked Italian-seasoned chicken sausage, cut into ¼-inch slices
- ½ teaspoon garlic powder
- ½ teaspoon ground black pepper
- 1 cup cherry tomatoes, cut in half
- 2 tablespoons finely sliced fresh basil leaves

PREPARE pasta according to package directions; drain.

MEANWHILE, COMBINE evaporated milk, cheese, sausage, garlic powder and black pepper in medium saucepan. Cook over medium-low heat, stirring occasionally, until cheese is melted. Remove from heat.

ADD pasta to cheese sauce; stir until combined. Add tomatoes and basil; stir gently until mixed in.

tip: Different flavors of chicken sausage can be substituted.

3-cheese mostaccioli bolognese
makes 6 servings

- 1 pound ground beef
- 2 cloves garlic, minced
- 1 medium zucchini, cut in half lengthwise and sliced (about 1 cup)
- 3 cups PREGO® Traditional Italian Sauce or PREGO® Organic Tomato & Basil Italian Sauce
- 6 cups mostaccioli or tube-shaped pasta (ziti), cooked and drained
- 6 ounces shredded mozzarella cheese (about 1½ cups)
- 1 cup ricotta cheese
- ¼ cup grated Parmesan cheese

1. Heat the oven to 400°F.

2. Cook the beef and garlic in a 12-inch skillet over medium-high heat until the beef is well browned, stirring often to break up the meat. Pour off any fat. Add the zucchini and cook until it's tender. Stir in the sauce.

3. Stir the beef mixture, pasta, ½ **cup** mozzarella cheese, ricotta cheese and Parmesan cheese in a 3-quart shallow baking dish. Sprinkle with the remaining mozzarella cheese.

4. Bake for 20 minutes or until the mixture is hot and bubbling and the cheese is melted.

prep time: 30 minutes • **cook time:** 20 minutes

polish reuben casserole

makes 8 to 10 servings

2 cans (10¾ ounces each) condensed cream of mushroom soup, undiluted

1⅓ cups milk

½ cup chopped onion

1 tablespoon prepared mustard

1 jar (32 ounces) sauerkraut, rinsed and drained

1 package (8 ounces) uncooked medium egg noodles

1½ pounds Polish sausage, cut into ½-inch pieces

2 cups (8 ounces) shredded Swiss cheese

¾ cup whole wheat bread crumbs

2 tablespoons butter, melted

1. Preheat oven to 350°F. Grease 13×9-inch baking dish.

2. Combine soup, milk, onion and mustard in medium bowl; stir well.

3. Spread sauerkraut in prepared dish. Top with noodles. Spoon soup mixture evenly over noodles; cover with sausage. Top with cheese.

4. Combine bread crumbs and butter in small bowl; sprinkle over casserole. Cover dish tightly with foil. Bake about 1 hour or until noodles are tender.

mediterranean mac & cheese
makes 4 to 6 servings

8 ounces uncooked elbow macaroni or other small pasta shape
1 tablespoon olive oil
1 red bell pepper, cut into slivers
1 bunch (about ¾ pound) asparagus, cut into bite-size pieces
4 tablespoons butter, divided
¼ cup all-purpose flour
1¾ cups milk, heated
1 teaspoon minced fresh thyme
Salt and black pepper
1 cup (4 ounces) shredded mozzarella cheese
1 cup bite-size pieces cooked chicken
4 ounces garlic and herb flavored goat cheese
¼ cup dry bread crumbs

1. Preheat oven to 350°F. Cook macaroni according to package directions until almost al dente. Rinse under cold running water to stop cooking; set aside.

2. Meanwhile, heat oil in medium skillet over medium-high heat; cook and stir bell pepper 3 minutes. Add asparagus; cook and stir 3 minutes or until crisp-tender. Remove from skillet.

3. Melt 3 tablespoons butter over medium-low heat in large saucepan or deep skillet until bubbly. Whisk in flour until smooth paste forms; cook and stir 2 minutes without browning. Gradually whisk in milk. Turn heat to medium; cook 6 to 8 minutes, whisking constantly until mixture begins to bubble and thickens slightly. Add thyme and season with salt and pepper. Remove from heat.

4. Stir in mozzarella cheese until melted. Add pasta, vegetables and chicken. Crumble goat cheese into mixture and transfer to 2-quart casserole dish. Top with bread crumbs and dot with remaining 1 tablespoon butter.

5. Bake 25 to 30 minutes or until lightly browned and bubbly.

no boiling mexicali mac & cheese bake

makes 8 servings

1 jar (1 pound) RAGÚ® Cheesy! Double Cheddar Sauce
1½ cups water
1 can (4 ounces) diced green chilies, undrained
1 cup chopped fresh tomatoes
1 cup (about 4 ounces) shredded Monterey Jack cheese, divided
8 ounces uncooked elbow macaroni

1. Preheat oven to 400°F.

2. In large bowl, combine Double Cheddar Sauce, water, chilies, tomatoes and ½ cup cheese. Stir in uncooked macaroni.

3. In 2-quart casserole, spoon macaroni mixture, then cover tightly with aluminum foil. Bake 45 minutes. Remove foil and sprinkle with remaining ½ cup cheese. Bake, uncovered, an additional 5 minutes. Let stand 5 minutes before serving.

prep time: 5 minutes • **cook time:** 50 minutes

pasta with four cheeses
makes 4 servings

¾ cup uncooked ziti or rigatoni
3 tablespoons butter, divided
½ cup grated CUCINA CLASSICA ITALIANA® Parmesan cheese, divided
¼ teaspoon ground nutmeg, divided
¼ cup GALBANI® Mascarpone
¾ cup (about 3½ ounces) shredded mozzarella cheese
¾ cup (about 3½ ounces) shredded BEL PAESE® semi-soft cheese

Preheat oven to 350°F. Lightly grease 1-quart casserole. Set aside.

In large saucepan of boiling water, cook pasta until tender but still firm. Drain in colander. Place in large mixing bowl. Stir in 1½ tablespoons butter, ¼ cup Parmesan cheese and ⅛ teaspoon nutmeg.

Spread one fourth of pasta mixture into prepared casserole. Spoon Mascarpone onto pasta. Layer with one fourth of pasta. Top with mozzarella. Add third layer of pasta. Sprinkle with Bel Paese® cheese. Top with remaining pasta. Dot with remaining 1½ tablespoons butter. Sprinkle with remaining ¼ cup Parmesan cheese and ⅛ teaspoon nutmeg. Bake until golden brown, about 20 minutes.

fettuccine gorgonzola with sun-dried tomatoes
makes 4 servings

- **4 ounces sun-dried tomatoes (not packed in oil)**
- **8 ounces uncooked spinach or tri-color fettuccine**
- **1 cup cottage cheese**
- **½ cup plain yogurt**
- **½ cup (2 ounces) crumbled Gorgonzola cheese, plus additional for garnish**
- **⅛ teaspoon white pepper**

1. Place sun-dried tomatoes in small bowl; pour hot water over to cover. Let stand 15 minutes or until tomatoes are soft. Drain well; cut into strips. Cook pasta according to package directions; drain well. Cover and keep warm.

2. Meanwhile, process cottage cheese and yogurt in food processor or blender until smooth. Heat cottage cheese mixture in large skillet over low heat. Add Gorgonzola cheese and white pepper; stir until cheese is melted.

3. Add pasta and tomatoes to skillet; toss to coat with sauce. Garnish with additional Gorgonzola cheese; serve immediately.

pasta with the works
makes 8 servings

1 package (1 pound) corkscrew-shaped pasta (rotini), cooked and drained (about 6 cups)

7½ cups PREGO® Traditional or PREGO® Roasted Garlic & Herb Italian Sauce

1 cup thinly sliced pepperoni, cut in half

2 medium green peppers, chopped (about 1½ cups)

1 cup large pitted ripe olives, cut in half

2 cups shredded mozzarella cheese (about 8 ounces)

Grated Parmesan cheese

1. Heat the pasta, Italian sauce, pepperoni, peppers, olives and mozzarella cheese in a 6-quart saucepot over medium heat until the mixture is hot and bubbling, stirring often.

2. Serve with the Parmesan cheese.

prep time: 15 minutes • **cook time:** 10 minutes

sun-dried tomato bow tie pasta
makes 4 servings

- 1 tablespoon olive oil
- 1 large onion, finely chopped (about 1 cup)
- ⅓ cup sun-dried tomatoes, cut into thin strips
- 2 cloves garlic, minced
- 1 can (10¾ ounces) CAMPBELL'S® Condensed Cream of Chicken Soup (Regular or 98% Fat Free)
- 1 cup milk
- 2 tablespoons thinly sliced fresh basil leaves
- 1 package (1 pound) bow tie pasta (farfalle) (about 6 cups), cooked and drained
- 2 tablespoons grated Parmesan cheese
- Freshly ground black pepper

1. Heat the oil in a 10-inch skillet over medium heat. Add the onion and cook until it's tender.

2. Add the tomatoes and garlic and cook for 1 minute. Stir the soup, milk and basil in the skillet. Cook until the mixture is hot and bubbling, stirring occasionally.

3. Place the pasta into a large serving bowl. Pour the soup mixture over the pasta and toss to coat. Sprinkle with the cheese. Season with the black pepper if desired.

tip: For a thinner sauce, reserve ¼ cup of the pasta cooking water and add it to the skillet with the soup and milk.

prep time: 10 minutes • **cook time:** 20 minutes

shrimp noodle supreme

makes 6 servings

1 package (8 ounces) spinach noodles,
   cooked and drained

1 package (3 ounces) cream cheese, cubed
   and softened

1½ pounds raw medium shrimp, peeled and
   deveined

½ cup (1 stick) butter, softened
   Salt and black pepper

1 can (10¾ ounces) condensed cream of mushroom soup,
   undiluted

1 cup sour cream

½ cup half-and-half

½ cup mayonnaise

1 tablespoon snipped chives, plus additional for garnish

1 tablespoon chopped fresh parsley, plus additional for garnish

½ teaspoon Dijon mustard

¾ cup (3 ounces) shredded sharp Cheddar cheese

1. Preheat oven to 325°F. Spray 13×9-inch casserole with nonstick
cooking spray.

2. Combine noodles and cream cheese in medium bowl. Spread
noodle mixture in prepared casserole. Melt butter in large skillet over
medium-high heat. Add shrimp; cook about 5 minutes or until pink
and opaque. Season to taste with salt and pepper. Layer shrimp over
noodles.

3. Combine soup, sour cream, half-and-half, mayonnaise, chives,
parsley and mustard in medium bowl. Spread over shrimp. Sprinkle
with Cheddar cheese.

4. Bake 25 minutes or until hot and cheese is melted. Sprinkle with
additional chives and parsley.

cheese lover's mac & cheese

makes 12 servings

1 pound uncooked elbow macaroni
¼ cup butter
¼ cup all-purpose flour
4 cups milk
½ teaspoon salt
4 cups (16 ounces) SARGENTO® Shredded
   Sharp Cheddar Cheese, divided
4 cups (16 ounces) SARGENTO® Shredded Mild Cheddar Cheese
2 cups (8 ounces) SARGENTO® Shredded Mozzarella Cheese,
   divided
8 ounces SARGENTO® Deli Style Sliced Muenster Cheese,
   divided
½ cup bread crumbs (optional)

COOK macaroni according to package directions. Meanwhile, melt
butter in a large saucepan over medium heat. Add flour; cook and stir
1 minute. Add milk and salt. Bring to a boil, stirring frequently. Reduce
heat; simmer 2 minutes or until sauce thickens. Stir in 3 cups sharp
Cheddar cheese and all of the mild Cheddar cheese until melted. Stir
in cooked macaroni.

SPREAD 4 cups macaroni mixture into two 8- or 9-inch baking
dishes or pans (or one of each). Layer 1 cup Mozzarella and half of
Muenster cheese slices over macaroni. Repeat layering with 4 cups
macaroni mixture, remaining 1 cup Mozzarella and Muenster cheese
slices. Spread remaining macaroni mixture over cheese; top with
remaining 1 cup sharp Cheddar cheese. Top with bread crumbs, if
desired.

BAKE in preheated 350°F oven 40 to 45 minutes or until bubbly.

prep time: 20 minutes • **cook time:** 45 minutes

pizza chicken bake

makes 4 servings

    3½ cups uncooked bowtie pasta
     1 tablespoon vegetable oil
     1 cup sliced mushrooms
     1 jar (26 ounces) pasta sauce with herbs
     1 teaspoon pizza seasoning blend
     3 boneless skinless chicken breasts (about ¾ pound), quartered
     1 cup (4 ounces) shredded mozzarella cheese

1. Preheat oven to 350°F. Spray 2-quart casserole with nonstick cooking spray. Cook pasta according to package directions until al dente. Drain and place in prepared dish.

2. Heat oil in large skillet over medium-high heat. Add mushrooms; cook and stir 2 minutes. Remove from heat. Stir in pasta sauce and pizza seasoning.

3. Pour half of sauce mixture into casserole; stir until pasta is well coated. Arrange chicken on top of pasta. Pour remaining sauce mixture evenly over chicken.

4. Bake, covered, 50 minutes or until chicken is no longer pink in center. Remove from oven; sprinkle with cheese. Cover and let stand 5 minutes before serving.

tip: Serve this casserole with grated Parmesan cheese and red pepper flakes so that everyone can add their own "pizza" seasonings.

tomato mac & cheese
makes 4 servings

  2 cups uncooked elbow macaroni
¼ cup butter
  3 tablespoons all-purpose flour
  1 teaspoon Italian seasoning
½ teaspoon black pepper
½ teaspoon salt
  2 cups milk
¼ cup (1 ounce) SARGENTO® Shredded
      Cheddar Cheese
¼ cup (1 ounce) SARGENTO® ARTISAN BLENDS™ Shredded
      Parmesan Cheese
  1 can (14½ ounces) diced tomatoes, drained
  1 cup (4 ounces) SARGENTO® Shredded Mozzarella Cheese
½ cup plain dry bread crumbs

PREHEAT oven to 350°F. Spray 2-quart baking dish with nonstick cooking spray.

COOK macaroni according to package directions until just tender. Drain and set aside.

MEANWHILE, melt butter in medium saucepan over medium heat. Whisk in flour, seasoning, pepper and salt, stirring until smooth. Gradually add milk, whisking constantly until slightly thickened. Add Cheddar and Parmesan; stir until smooth.

LAYER half of pasta, half of tomatoes and half of cheese sauce in prepared baking dish. Repeat layers.

SPRINKLE Mozzarella cheese evenly over casserole. Place bread crumbs in small bowl; spray several times with cooking spray. Sprinkle over pasta mixture.

BAKE, covered, 30 minutes or until hot and bubbly. Uncover and bake 5 minutes or until top is golden brown.

prep time: 10 minutes • **cook time:** 50 minutes

ham and cheese pasta bake

makes 6 servings

  6 cups water
12 ounces uncooked rigatoni pasta
  2 teaspoons salt
  1 ham steak, cubed
  1 container (10 ounces) refrigerated
      Alfredo sauce
  2 cups (8 ounces) mozzarella cheese, divided
  2 cups half-and-half, warmed
  1 tablespoon cornstarch

slow cooker directions

1. Bring water to a boil in large saucepan over high heat. Add rigatoni and salt; cook 7 minutes. Drain well; transfer to slow cooker.

2. Stir in ham, Alfredo sauce and 1 cup cheese. Whisk half-and-half and cornstarch in medium bowl; pour over pasta. Sprinkle with remaining cheese. Cover; cook on LOW 3½ to 4 hours or until rigatoni is tender and excess liquid is absorbed.

prep time: 15 minutes • **cook time:** 3½ to 4 hours

veggie mac and tuna
makes 6 servings

1½ cups (6 ounces) elbow macaroni
3 tablespoons butter or margarine
1 small onion, chopped
½ medium red bell pepper, chopped
½ medium green bell pepper, chopped
¼ cup all-purpose flour
1¾ cups milk
8 ounces cubed pasteurized process cheese product
½ teaspoon dried marjoram
1 package (10 ounces) frozen peas
1 can (9 ounces) tuna in water, drained

slow cooker directions

1. Cook macaroni according to package directions until just tender; drain.

2. Melt butter in medium saucepan over medium heat. Add onion and bell peppers; cook and stir 5 minutes or until tender. Whisk in flour until smooth paste forms; cook 2 minutes without browning. Stir in milk. Bring to a boil. Boil, stirring constantly, until thickened. Reduce heat to low; add cheese and marjoram. Stir until cheese is melted.

3. Combine macaroni, cheese sauce, peas and tuna in slow cooker. Cover and cook on LOW 2½ hours or until bubbly at edge.

hearty noodle casserole
makes 4 to 6 servings

  1 pound Italian sausage, casings removed
  1 jar (26½ ounces) pasta sauce
  2 cups (16 ounces) ricotta or cottage cheese
  **1 package (12 ounces) extra wide egg noodles, cooked and
    drained**
  2 cups (8 ounces) shredded mozzarella cheese, divided
  1 can (4 ounces) sliced mushrooms
  ½ cup chopped green bell pepper

1. Preheat oven to 350°F. Brown sausage in large skillet over medium-high heat 6 to 8 minutes, stirring to break up meat. Drain fat.

2. Combine sausage, pasta sauce, ricotta cheese, noodles, half of mozzarella cheese, mushrooms and bell pepper in large bowl. Spoon into 13×9-inch baking dish or 3-quart casserole. Top with remaining mozzarella cheese.

3. Bake 25 minutes or until heated through.

mom's baked mostaccioli

makes 8 servings

1 container (15 ounces) ricotta cheese
2 eggs, lightly beaten
¼ cup grated Parmesan cheese
1 teaspoon Italian seasoning
½ teaspoon garlic powder
½ teaspoon black pepper
1 package (16 ounces) mostaccioli, cooked
   and drained
1 jar (26 ounces) pasta sauce
1½ cups (6 ounces) shredded mozzarella cheese

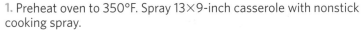

1. Preheat oven to 350°F. Spray 13×9-inch casserole with nonstick cooking spray.

2. Combine ricotta cheese, eggs and Parmesan cheese in medium bowl. Season with garlic powder, pepper and Italian seasoning; mix well.

3. Place half of pasta and half of sauce in prepared casserole. Spread ricotta mixture evenly over pasta. Spoon remaining pasta and sauce over ricotta mixture. Top with mozzarella cheese.

4. Bake 30 minutes or until hot and bubbly.

three-cheese penne
makes 6 servings

Nonstick cooking spray
2 cups (about 6½ ounces) uncooked penne pasta
2 slices whole wheat bread, cut into cubes
2 cups (16 ounces) cottage cheese
2 cups (8 ounces) shredded Cheddar cheese
1 cup chopped plum tomatoes, divided
⅓ cup sliced green onions
¼ cup grated Parmesan cheese
¼ cup milk

1. Preheat oven to 350°F. Spray 2-quart casserole with nonstick cooking spray. Cook pasta according to package directions. Rinse under cold running water until pasta is cool; set aside.

2. Spray large nonstick skillet with cooking spray; heat over medium heat. Place bread cubes in skillet; spray bread cubes lightly with cooking spray. Cook and stir 5 minutes or until bread cubes are browned and crisp.

3. Combine pasta, cottage cheese, Cheddar cheese, ¾ cup tomatoes, green onions, Parmesan cheese and milk in medium bowl. Place pasta mixture in prepared casserole. Top with remaining ¼ cup tomatoes and bread cubes.

4. Bake 20 minutes or until heated through.

mac & cheese pizza

makes 4 to 6 servings

1½ **tablespoons unsalted butter**
1½ **tablespoons all-purpose flour**
  1 **cup half-and-half or milk, heated**
 ¼ **teaspoon salt**
 ¼ **teaspoon black pepper**
 ¼ **teaspoon dried oregano**
 ½ **cup shredded fontina cheese**
 ½ **cup shredded Parmesan cheese**
  3 **cups cooked* macaroni (about 1½ cups uncooked)**
  1 **tablespoon olive oil**
  1 **cup sliced mushrooms**
  8 **ounces bulk Italian sausage**
  1 **cup marinara sauce**
  1 **cup (4 ounces) shredded mozzarella cheese**

*Cook macaroni until very tender, a bit longer than for al dente.

1. Preheat oven to 350°F. Spray 10-inch round deep-dish pizza pan, tart pan or shallow casserole with cooking spray.

2. Melt butter in large saucepan or deep skillet over medium-low heat until bubbly. Whisk in flour until smooth paste forms. Gradually add half-and-half, whisking until thickened. Add salt, pepper and oregano. Gradually stir in fontina and Parmesan cheeses until melted. Stir in macaroni. Spoon into prepared pan. Press down firmly into even layer. Bake 15 minutes. Set aside.

3. Meanwhile, heat oil in large skillet over medium heat. Add mushrooms; cook 5 minutes, stirring occasionally. Add sausage, breaking into bite-size pieces with back of spoon. Cook over medium-high heat until browned, stirring occasionally; drain fat. Stir in marinara sauce and cook 1 minute or until heated through.

4. Spread sauce mixture evenly over macaroni layer. Sprinkle with mozzarella cheese. Bake 15 to 20 minutes or until bubbly and cheese melts. Let stand 5 minutes before slicing.

cousin arlene's spaghetti lasagna

makes 6 servings

8 ounces uncooked spaghetti
1 tablespoon butter
1 clove garlic, minced
2 pounds ground beef
1 teaspoon sugar
   Salt and black pepper
2 cans (8 ounces each) tomato sauce
1 can (6 ounces) tomato paste
1 cup (8 ounces) sour cream
3 ounces cream cheese, softened
6 green onions, chopped
¼ cup grated Parmesan cheese

1. Preheat oven to 350°F. Cook spaghetti according to package directions; drain.

2. Meanwhile, melt butter in large skillet over medium heat. Add garlic; cook and stir 1 minute. Add ground beef, sugar, salt and pepper. Brown beef 6 to 8 minutes, stirring to break up meat; drain fat. Add tomato sauce and tomato paste; simmer 20 minutes, stirring occasionally.

3. Meanwhile, beat sour cream and cream cheese in medium bowl until smooth. Stir in green onions.

4. Spread ½ cup meat sauce in 2-quart casserole. Layer with half of spaghetti, half of sour cream mixture and half of remaining meat sauce. Repeat layers. Sprinkle with Parmesan cheese. Bake 35 minutes or until heated through.

tip: This casserole can be frozen. Thaw it in the refrigerator overnight, then let it come to room temperature before baking. Bake until it is heated through. This recipe can also be doubled to make great leftovers.

mac and cheese mini cups

makes 36 mini cups

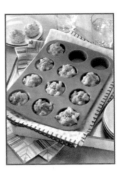

3 tablespoons butter, divided
2 tablespoons all-purpose flour
1 cup milk
1 teaspoon salt
½ teaspoon black pepper
1 cup (4 ounces) shredded sharp Cheddar
   cheese
1 cup (4 ounces) shredded Muenster
   cheese
½ pound elbow macaroni, cooked and drained
⅓ cup plain dry bread crumbs

1. Preheat oven to 400°F. Melt 1 tablespoon butter in large saucepan over medium heat; grease 36 mini (1¾-inch) muffin cups with melted butter.

2. Melt remaining 2 tablespoons butter in same saucepan over medium heat. Whisk in flour until smooth paste forms; cook 2 minutes without browning. Add milk, salt and pepper; whisk 3 minutes or until thickened. Remove from heat; gradually stir in cheeses. Fold in macaroni. Divide mixture among prepared muffin cups; sprinkle with bread crumbs.

3. Bake 20 minutes or until golden brown. Cool in pans 10 minutes; carefully remove from pans using knife.

salmon & noodle casserole
makes 4 to 5 servings

6 ounces uncooked wide noodles
1 teaspoon vegetable oil
1 medium onion, finely chopped
¾ cup thinly sliced carrot
¾ cup thinly sliced celery
1 can (about 15 ounces) salmon, drained, skin and bones discarded
1 can (10¾ ounces) cream of celery soup, undiluted
1 cup (4 ounces) shredded Cheddar cheese
¾ cup frozen peas
½ cup sour cream
¼ cup milk
2 teaspoons dried dill weed
Black pepper
Chopped fresh dill (optional)

1. Preheat oven to 350°F. Cook noodles in large saucepan according to package directions. Drain and return to saucepan.

2. Meanwhile, heat oil in large skillet over medium heat. Add onion, carrot and celery; cook and stir 4 to 5 minutes or until carrot is crisp-tender.

3. Add salmon, onion mixture, soup, cheese, peas, sour cream, milk, dill weed and pepper to noodles; stir gently until blended. Pour into 2-quart casserole dish.

4. Cover and bake 25 to 30 minutes or until hot and bubbly. Garnish with fresh dill.

easy & cheesy

tuna-macaroni casserole
makes 6 servings

> 1 cup mayonnaise
> 1 cup (4 ounces) shredded Swiss cheese
> ½ cup milk
> ¼ cup chopped onion
> ¼ cup chopped red bell pepper
> ⅛ teaspoon black pepper
> 2 cans (7 ounces each) tuna, drained and flaked
> 1 package (about 10 ounces) frozen peas
> 2 cups shell pasta or elbow macaroni, cooked and drained
> ½ cup dry bread crumbs
> 2 tablespoons melted butter

1. Preheat oven to 350°F.

2. Combine mayonnaise, cheese, milk, onion, bell pepper and black pepper in large bowl. Add tuna, peas and macaroni, toss to coat well. Spoon into 2-quart casserole.

3. Mix bread crumbs with butter in small bowl and sprinkle over top of casserole. Bake 30 to 40 minutes or until heated through.

two cheese macaroni bake

makes 6 servings

- **2 tablespoons butter**
- **2½ tablespoons all-purpose flour**
- **2 cups milk**
- **¾ teaspoon salt**
- **⅛ teaspoon cayenne pepper**
- **8 ounces elbow macaroni, mostaccioli or penne pasta, cooked and drained**
- **4 slices SARGENTO® Deli Style Sliced Monterey Jack Cheese**
- **6 slices SARGENTO® Deli Style Sliced Medium Cheddar Cheese**
  Paprika (optional)

MELT butter in medium saucepan over medium heat. Stir in flour until smooth; cook 1 minute, stirring constantly. Stir in milk, salt and cayenne pepper. Heat to a boil; reduce heat. Simmer 1 minute or until thickened, stirring frequently. Stir in pasta.

SPOON half of pasta mixture into 8×8-inch square pan; top with Monterey Jack cheese. Repeat with remaining pasta and Cheddar cheese. Sprinkle with paprika, if desired. Bake in preheated 375°F oven 25 minutes or until bubbly.

prep time: 15 minutes • **cook time:** 27 minutes

extra-easy spinach lasagna
makes 8 servings

1 container (15 ounces) ricotta cheese
1 package (10 ounces) frozen chopped spinach, thawed and well drained
8 ounces shredded mozzarella cheese (about 2 cups)
1 jar (24 ounces) PREGO® Fresh Mushroom Italian Sauce
6 uncooked lasagna noodles
¼ cup water

1. Stir the ricotta cheese, spinach and 1 cup mozzarella cheese in a medium bowl.

2. Spread **1 cup** Italian sauce in a 2-quart shallow baking dish. Top with **3** lasagna noodles and **half** the spinach mixture. Repeat the layers. Top with the remaining sauce. Slowly pour water around the inside edges of the baking dish. **Cover.**

3. Bake at 400°F. for 40 minutes. Uncover the dish. Sprinkle with the remaining mozzarella cheese. Bake for 10 minutes or until it's hot and bubbling. Let stand for 10 minutes.

kitchen tip: To thaw the spinach, microwave on HIGH for 3 minutes, breaking apart with a fork halfway through heating.

prep time: 20 minutes • **cook time:** 1 hour

quick skillet chicken & macaroni parmesan

makes 6 servings

   1 jar (1 pound 10 ounces) PREGO® Traditional Italian Sauce
   ¼ cup grated Parmesan cheese, divided
   3 cups cubed cooked chicken
   1½ cups elbow macaroni, cooked and drained
   1½ cups shredded part-skim mozzarella cheese (6 ounces)

1. Heat the Italian sauce, **3 tablespoons** of the Parmesan cheese, chicken and macaroni in a 10-inch skillet over medium-high heat to a boil. Reduce the heat to medium. Cover and cook for 10 minutes or until the mixture is hot and bubbling, stirring occasionally.

2. Sprinkle with the mozzarella cheese and remaining Parmesan cheese. Let stand for 5 minutes or until the cheese melts.

tip: Use 1½ pounds skinless, boneless chicken breasts, cut into cubes for the cooked chicken. Heat 1 tablespoon olive oil in a 12-inch skillet over medium-high heat. Add the chicken in 2 batches and cook until it's well browned, stirring often. Continue to cook, proceeding as directed in step 1 above.

prep time: 15 minutes • **cook time:** 15 minutes

ham & cheese shells & trees

makes 4 servings

2 tablespoons margarine or butter
1 (6.2-ounce) package PASTA RONI®
   Shells & White Cheddar
2 cups fresh or frozen chopped broccoli
⅔ cup milk
1½ cups ham or cooked turkey, cut into thin
   strips (about 6 ounces)

1. In large saucepan, bring 2 cups water and margarine to a boil.

2. Stir in pasta. Reduce heat to medium. Gently boil, uncovered, 6 minutes, stirring occasionally. Stir in broccoli; return to a boil. Boil 6 to 8 minutes or until most of water is absorbed.

3. Stir in milk, ham and Special Seasonings. Return to a boil; boil 1 to 2 minutes or until pasta is tender. Let stand 5 minutes before serving.

tip: No leftovers? Ask the deli to slice a ½-inch-thick piece of ham or turkey.

prep time: 5 minutes • **cook time:** 20 minutes

mac & mexican four cheese
makes 8 servings

1 pound uncooked fusilli, rotelle or elbow pasta
1 jar (16 ounces) PACE® Mexican Four Cheese Salsa con Queso
1 can (about 14.5 ounces) diced tomatoes, drained
4 green onions, sliced (about ½ cup)
1 cup crushed tortilla chips

1. Cook the pasta in a 6-quart saucepan according to the package directions. Drain. Return the pasta to the saucepan. Add the queso, tomatoes and green onions. Cook over medium heat for 5 minutes or until the pasta mixture is hot, stirring often.

2. Top with the tortilla chips before serving.

tip: When cooking pasta, make sure to bring the water to a full boil before adding a generous sprinkling of salt to flavor the pasta. Stir the pasta once you put it in so it doesn't stick, but it doesn't need stirring once the water resumes its full boil.

total time: 20 minutes

today's macaroni & cheese
makes 8 servings

    2 cups milk
    4 tablespoons butter or margarine
    ¼ cup all-purpose flour
    2 cups chunky-style salsa
 1½ teaspoons salt
    3 cups (12 ounces) SARGENTO® Fancy Shredded 4 Cheese
       Mexican Cheese
    1 pound pasta (elbow macaroni, cork-screw or rotini), cooked,
       drained and warm
    ¼ cup chopped fresh cilantro

WARM milk in small saucepan over medium heat or in microwave oven.

MELT butter in medium saucepan over medium heat. Stir in flour and whisk 2 minutes until mixture becomes golden in color. Add warmed milk; continue to whisk until mixture thickens and comes to a full boil. Stir in salsa and salt; remove from heat. Stir in cheese until melted.

POUR cheese sauce over pasta and spoon into serving dish. Sprinkle with cilantro and serve hot.

prep time: 20 minutes • **cook time:** 15 minutes

wisconsin cheese pasta casserole
makes 6 to 8 servings

1 pound spaghetti or fettuccine, broken into 3-inch pieces
1 quart (4 cups) prepared spaghetti sauce
½ cup plus ⅓ cup grated Wisconsin Romano cheese, divided
1¾ cups (7 ounces) sliced or shredded Wisconsin Colby cheese
1½ cups (6 ounces) shredded Wisconsin Mozzarella cheese

Prepare pasta according to package instructions; drain. Toss warm pasta with prepared spaghetti sauce to coat. Add ½ cup Romano cheese to mixture and mix well. Spread half of sauced pasta into bottom of 13×9×2-inch baking dish. Cover with 1 cup Colby cheese. Spread remaining pasta over cheese. Top with remaining ¾ cup Colby cheese. Sprinkle with remaining ⅓ cup Romano cheese and Mozzarella cheese. Bake at 350°F for 35 to 40 minutes or until top is lightly browned and casserole is bubbly. Remove from heat and let stand at least 10 minutes before serving.

*Favorite recipe from **Wisconsin Milk Marketing Board***

salsa macaroni & cheese
makes 4 servings

1 jar (1 pound) RAGÚ® Cheesy! Double Cheddar Sauce
1 cup mild salsa
8 ounces elbow macaroni, cooked and drained

Heat Double Cheddar Sauce in 2-quart saucepan over medium heat. Stir in salsa; heat through. Toss with hot macaroni.

tip: Also fun with wagon wheel pasta!

prep time: 20 minutes • **cook time:** 10 minutes

chicken noodle casserole
make 4 to 6 servings

1 package (12 ounces) wide egg noodles
2 cups chopped cooked chicken
**1 can (10¾ ounces) condensed cream of mushroom soup,
undiluted**
1 cup (4 ounces) shredded Cheddar-Jack cheese
½ cup sour cream
½ cup milk
⅓ to ½ cup dry bread crumbs
1 to 2 tablespoons fresh parsley (optional)

1. Preheat oven to 350°F. Spray 13×9-inch baking dish with nonstick cooking spray.

2. Cook noodles according to package directions; drain. Return to saucepan. Add chicken, soup, cheese, sour cream and milk; mix well. Transfer to prepared baking dish; top with bread crumbs.

3. Bake 25 minutes or until hot and bubbly. Garnish with parsley.

tip: Leftover cooked chicken is perfect for this recipe, but if you don't have any on hand, a 3-pound chicken will yield about 3 cups of meat, after cooking, boning and chopping. Or, if you'd prefer only white meat, 1 to 1¼ pounds of boneless skinless chicken breasts will yield about 3 cups.

velveeta® ultimate macaroni & cheese
makes 4 servings

  2 cups elbow macaroni, uncooked
  ¾ pound (12 ounces) VELVEETA® Pasteurized Prepared Cheese Product, cut into ½-inch cubes
  ⅓ cup milk
  ⅛ teaspoon black pepper

1. COOK macaroni in large saucepan as directed on package; drain well. Return to pan.

2. STIR in remaining ingredients; cook on low heat until VELVEETA® is completely melted and mixture is well blended, stirring frequently.

tip: Save 70 calories and 10 grams of fat per serving by preparing with VELVEETA® Made With 2% Milk Reduced Fat Pasteurized Prepared Cheese Product.

variation: Prepare as directed. Pour into 2-quart casserole dish. Bake at 350°F for 25 minutes.

dressed-up mac 'n cheese: Substitute bow tie pasta or your favorite shaped pasta for the macaroni.

prep time: 5 minutes • **total time:** 20 minutes

easy cheese & tomato macaroni

makes 6 to 8 servings

2 packages (7 ounces each) macaroni and cheese dinner
1 tablespoon olive or vegetable oil
1 cup finely chopped onion
2 cups thinly sliced celery
1 can (28 ounces) CONTADINA® Crushed Tomatoes
   Grated Parmesan cheese (optional)
   Sliced green onion or celery leaves (optional)

1. Cook macaroni (from macaroni and cheese dinner) according to package directions; drain.

2. Heat oil in large skillet. Add chopped onion and celery; sauté for 3 minutes or until vegetables are tender.

3. Combine tomatoes and cheese mixes from dinners in small bowl. Stir into vegetable mixture.

4. Simmer for 3 to 4 minutes or until mixture is thickened and heated through. Add macaroni to skillet; stir until well coated with sauce. Heat thoroughly, stirring occasionally. Sprinkle with Parmesan cheese and sliced green onion, if desired.

easy cheesy lasagna
makes 6 servings

2 tablespoons olive oil
3 small zucchini, thinly sliced
1 package (8 ounces) mushrooms, thinly sliced
1 medium onion, chopped
5 cloves garlic, minced
2 containers (15 ounces each) ricotta cheese
2 eggs
¼ cup grated Parmesan cheese
½ teaspoon Italian seasoning
¼ teaspoon garlic salt
⅛ teaspoon black pepper
1 can (28 ounces) crushed tomatoes in purée
1 jar (26 ounces) pasta sauce
1 package (16 ounces) uncooked lasagna noodles
4 cups (16 ounces) shredded mozzarella cheese, divided

1. Preheat oven to 375°F. Spray 13×9-inch baking dish with nonstick cooking spray.

2. Heat oil in large skillet over medium heat. Cook and stir zucchini, mushrooms, onion and garlic 5 minutes or until tender.

3. Combine ricotta cheese, eggs, Parmesan cheese, Italian seasoning, garlic salt and pepper in medium bowl. Combine tomatoes and pasta sauce in another medium bowl.

4. Spread one third of tomato mixture in prepared dish. Layer with one third of noodles. Spread half of vegetable mixture over noodles; top with half of ricotta mixture. Sprinkle with 1 cup mozzarella. Layer one third of noodles over mozzarella. Top with one third of tomato mixture and remaining vegetable and ricotta cheese mixtures. Sprinkle with 1 cup mozzarella. Layer one third of noodles over mozzarella; spread with remaining tomato mixture and sprinkle with remaining 2 cups mozzarella.

5. Cover with foil; bake 1 hour or until noodles are soft. Uncover; bake 5 minutes or until cheese is melted and lightly browned.

creole macaroni and cheese

makes 4 to 6 servings

½ cup butter or margarine
1 package (12 ounces) uncooked elbow macaroni
1 can (14½ ounces) DEL MONTE® Diced Tomatoes with Onion & Garlic
1 teaspoon salt
½ teaspoon white pepper
1 tablespoon flour
1 can (12 fluid ounces) evaporated milk
2 cups shredded sharp Cheddar cheese

1. Melt butter in large skillet. Add macaroni, tomatoes, salt and pepper. Cook 5 minutes, stirring occasionally.

2. Add 1½ cups water; bring to a boil. Cover and simmer 20 minutes or until macaroni is tender.

3. Sprinkle in flour; blend well. Stir in evaporated milk until blended. Stir in cheese. Simmer 5 minutes, stirring occasionally, until cheese is completely melted. Garnish with green pepper or parsley, if desired. Serve immediately.

prep & cook time: 35 minutes

acknowledgments

The publisher would like to thank the companies and organizations
listed below for the use of their recipes and photographs
in this publication.

BelGioioso® Cheese Inc.

Cabot® Creamery Cooperative

Campbell Soup Company

Cucina Classica Italiana, Inc.

Del Monte Foods

The Golden Grain Company®

Hillshire Farm®

®Johnsonville Sausage, LLC

Kraft Foods Global, Inc.

McIlhenny Company (TABASCO® brand Pepper Sauce)

Nestlé USA

Reckitt Benckiser LLC.

Recipes courtesy of the Reynolds Kitchens

Sargento® Foods Inc.

StarKist®

Tyson Foods, Inc.

Unilever

Wisconsin Milk Marketing Board

A

Artichoke-Olive Chicken Bake, 40

B

Baked Pasta and Cheese Supreme, 10

Baked Pasta Primavera Casserole, 73

Baked Ziti, 20

Beef, Bean and Pasta Casserole, 28

Beefy Pasta Casserole, 44

Broccoli & Cheese Stuffed Shells, 54

Broccoli Mac & Cheese, 72

C

Catalonian Stew, 90

Cheddar Brat Mac and Cheese, 35

Cheddar & Cavatappi, 16

Cheddar Tuna Noodles, 7

Cheeseburger Macaroni, 47

Cheeseburger Pasta 'n Vegetables Dinner, 43

Cheese Lover's Mac & Cheese, 103

Cheesy Italian Pasta Bake, 80

Cheesy Spinach Bake, 58

Cheesy Turkey Twists, 39

Chicken-Asparagus Casserole, 62

Chicken & Broccoli Alfredo, 82

Chicken Noodle Casserole, 132

Chili Spaghetti Casserole, 36

Classic Chicken Tetrazzini, 87

Classic Macaroni and Cheese, 4

Confetti Mac & Cheese, 15

Cousin Arlene's Spaghetti Lasagna, 116

Crab-Artichoke Casserole, 69

Creamy Chicken and Pasta with Spinach, 56

Creole Macaroni and Cheese, 140

Crowd Pleasin' Cheesy Sausage Ziti, 42

E

Easy Cheese & Tomato Macaroni, 136

Easy Cheesy Lasagna, 138

Easy Pumpkin-Pasta Bake, 57

Extra-Easy Spinach Lasagna, 123

F

Fettuccine Gorgonzola with Sun-Dried Tomatoes, 98

G

Garden Vegetable Lasagna, 61

Greek Skillet Lasagna, 88

H

Ham and Cheese Pasta Bake, 107

Ham & Cheese Shells & Trees, 126

Hearty Beef Lasagna, 32

Hearty Noodle Casserole, 110

Home-Style Macaroni and Cheese, 24

I

Italian Mac & Cheese, 77

Italian-Style Mac & Cheese with Chicken Sausage, 91

Italian Three-Cheese Macaroni, 86

K

Kale, Gorgonzola & Noodle Casserole, 70

Kielbasa and Broccoli Linguine, 31

M

Mac and Cheese Mini Cups, 117

Mac & Cheese Pizza, 114

Mac & Cheesiest, 8

Mac & Mexican Four Cheese, 127

Macaroni and Cheese Dijon, 12

Macaroni & Cheese with Bacon & Tomatoes, 6

Macaroni-Stuffed Peppers, 66

Mediterranean Mac & Cheese, 94

Mom's Baked Mostaccioli, 112

N

No Boiling Mexicali Mac & Cheese Bake, 96
Now & Later Baked Ziti, 83

O

Old-Fashioned Macaroni & Cheese with Broccoli, 65

P

Pasta with Four Cheeses, 97
Pasta with Onions and Goat Cheese, 76
Pasta with the Works, 99
Penne with Sausage and Feta, 60
Pepper Jack Cheesy Mac, 23
Pizza Chicken Bake, 104
Polish Reuben Casserole, 93

Q

Quick Skillet Chicken & Macaroni Parmesan, 124

R

Reuben Noodle Bake, 78
Roasted Garlic & Stout Mac & Cheese, 14

S

Salmon & Noodle Casserole, 118
Salsa Macaroni & Cheese, 131
Shells & Fontina, 74
Shrimp Noodle Supreme, 102
South-of-the-Border Macaroni & Cheese, 81
Southwestern Mac and Cheese, 19
Spicy Chili Mac, 38
Spicy Ham & Cheese Pasta, 30
Spicy Macaroni and Cheese with Broccoli, 50
Sun-Dried Tomato Bow Tie Pasta, 100

T

3-Cheese Chicken Penne Pasta Bake, 18
Three-Cheese Mostaccioli Bolognese, 92
3-Cheese Pasta Bake, 26
Three-Cheese Penne, 113
Today's Macaroni & Cheese, 128
Tofu Rigatoni Casserole, 68
Tomato, Brie & Noodle Casserole, 84
Tomato Mac & Cheese, 106
Traditional Macaroni & Cheese, 11
Tuna-Macaroni Casserole, 120
Tuna Tomato Casserole, 53
Turkey Veggie Tetrazzini, 52
Two Cheese Macaroni Bake, 122

V

Veg•All® Beef & Cheddar Bake, 27
Veggie Mac and Tuna, 108
Velveeta® Down-Home Macaroni & Cheese, 22
Velveeta® Italian Sausage Bake, 48
Velveeta® Sausage and Rice Casserole, 48
Velveeta® Ultimate Macaroni & Cheese, 134
Vermont Harvest Mac-n-Cheese, 46

W

Wisconsin Cheese Pasta Casserole, 130
Wisconsin Swiss Ham and Noodles Casserole, 34

Z

Zucchini and Mushroom Lasagna with Tofu, 64

metric conversion chart

VOLUME MEASUREMENTS (dry)

1/8 teaspoon = 0.5 mL
1/4 teaspoon = 1 mL
1/2 teaspoon = 2 mL
3/4 teaspoon = 4 mL
1 teaspoon = 5 mL
1 tablespoon = 15 mL
2 tablespoons = 30 mL
1/4 cup = 60 mL
1/3 cup = 75 mL
1/2 cup = 125 mL
2/3 cup = 150 mL
3/4 cup = 175 mL
1 cup = 250 mL
2 cups = 1 pint = 500 mL
3 cups = 750 mL
4 cups = 1 quart = 1 L

VOLUME MEASUREMENTS (fluid)

1 fluid ounce (2 tablespoons) = 30 mL
4 fluid ounces (1/2 cup) = 125 mL
8 fluid ounces (1 cup) = 250 mL
12 fluid ounces (1 1/2 cups) = 375 mL
16 fluid ounces (2 cups) = 500 mL

WEIGHTS (mass)

1/2 ounce = 15 g
1 ounce = 30 g
3 ounces = 90 g
4 ounces = 120 g
8 ounces = 225 g
10 ounces = 285 g
12 ounces = 360 g
16 ounces = 1 pound = 450 g

DIMENSIONS

1/16 inch = 2 mm
1/8 inch = 3 mm
1/4 inch = 6 mm
1/2 inch = 1.5 cm
3/4 inch = 2 cm
1 inch = 2.5 cm

OVEN TEMPERATURES

250°F = 120°C
275°F = 140°C
300°F = 150°C
325°F = 160°C
350°F = 180°C
375°F = 190°C
400°F = 200°C
425°F = 220°C
450°F = 230°C

BAKING PAN SIZES

Utensil	Size in Inches/Quarts	Metric Volume	Size in Centimeters
Baking or Cake Pan (square or rectangular)	8 × 8 × 2	2 L	20 × 20 × 5
	9 × 9 × 2	2.5 L	23 × 23 × 5
	12 × 8 × 2	3 L	30 × 20 × 5
	13 × 9 × 2	3.5 L	33 × 23 × 5
Loaf Pan	8 × 4 × 3	1.5 L	20 × 10 × 7
	9 × 5 × 3	2 L	23 × 13 × 7
Round Layer Cake Pan	8 × 1 1/2	1.2 L	20 × 4
	9 × 1 1/2	1.5 L	23 × 4
Pie Plate	8 × 1 1/4	750 mL	20 × 3
	9 × 1 1/4	1 L	23 × 3
Baking Dish or Casserole	1 quart	1 L	—
	1 1/2 quart	1.5 L	—
	2 quart	2 L	—